BETTER THAN SANE

BETTER THAN SANE

Tales from a Dangling Girl

Alison Rose

Alfred A. Knopf New York 2004

Knopf, Borzoi Books, and the colophon are registered trademarks
of Random House, Inc.

Library of Congress Catalogue-in-Publication Data
Rose, Alison (Alison C.)
Better than sane / Alison Rose.—1st ed.
p. cm.
ISBN 1-4000-4124-4 (alk. paper)
1. Rose, Alison (Alison C.)—Childhood and youth. 2. Journalists—
United States—Biography. I. Title.
PN4874.R587A3 2004
070.92—dc22
[B]   2003060245

Manufactured in the United States of America

First Edition

For my mother

You are, you know, you were the nearest
thing to a real story to happen in my life.

—RENATA ADLER

CONTENTS

ACKNOWLEDGEMENTS

To Elizabeth Macklin and to Linda Asher, John Bennet, and Jin. And, of course, Vicky Wilson. Thank you.

BETTER THAN SANE

MY ROOM ALONE, WITH ANIMALS

I n my room, on East Sixty-eighth Street in New York City, there's the same oval mirror that I looked in when I was growing up in California. It's fake French. The ceiling is high, and two huge sets of windows on one side of the room are made up of small rectangles of pastel-colored glass. The walls are painted pink, and the ceiling is white—the room looks like a cake.

A man I had a lot of—or some—sex with there, a doleful rock-and-roll icon with the prettiest mouth (his music is still upsettingly on the radio all the time), told me that the room looked like New Orleans. A big quilt given to me in 1970 by a man I knew in Los Angeles hangs above a refectory table with three lamps on it and also a blue typewriter. There's a green wicker chair with chintz cushions; my cat used to sit on it. The head of my bed is pushed against the middle of one wall; on one side of the bed, there's a round table with photographs of the cat, Toast, and of my dog, Puppy Jane, on it. I used to have a little collection of photographs of men—a set of boyfriends I had once—on that table, but I took them off and stashed them in a drawer, after some deliberation.

The table on the other side of my bed has a blue vase on it with dried peonies all shoved together; and my dark-red hymnal from the Annie Wright Seminary; and a navy-blue Book of Common Prayer that George Trow gave me when we were friends. There's a footstool from my childhood room, and parquet floors that I like, and a big old rug the colors of the windows. There's a framed pale-blue horse that Billy the Fish made at the kitchen table in West Hollywood thirty-two years ago, when we lived together. A while ago now, Monique, my French friend, made a bright-blue tissue-paper sky with tinfoil stars in it and stuck it under the frame above the horse because she thought the horse looked *triste*. On the floor, leaning against the wall, is a photograph of me from 1977. A few weeks ago, a man I have a thing about these days—I forced him to come into my room for just a minute to look around—saw it and said, "You look noble." I do.

Inside one of my closets are seven shopping bags full of pieces of paper with sacred things written on them by men I've known, and then two boxes of drafts and photocopies of letters I wrote to them, neatly tied up with good-looking string. The other closet has mostly black clothes in it. There are tapes and CDs all over the floor by the bed and, in frames on different walls, four drawings by Harold Brodkey, perhaps the king of all my old boyfriends; a gold paper star that George, who was my absolute favorite, gave me one Christmas; and a drawing by another man of Puppy Jane attempting to fly too close to the sun. She looks like me in it. In one of Harold's drawings, there's a very small bird flying toward a birdhouse in a tree. The title he gave it is "Wow! A Happy Ending!" Another drawing of his, of me, or my face, has a typewritten comment from him on it:

> There should be a Bureau of Metropolitan Longing to explain to you why your life doesn't mean more than it does and why you don't have a lover who is your equal in devotion and the ability to do his work.

People can come into my room if I invite them, but if they don't like it they can get out fast, because it's *my room*. Everything that's in it is my private collection of my whole life: the good stuff. What I think and have thought and the aura of other people who've been in there and the rooms I've had before this one—everything in my room that shows, and a lot that doesn't, is self-sufficiently important. It eradicates the bad stuff that has threatened to define me all my life, when I look around at it. Most of the framed things on the walls have to do with people I've known who still matter to me. Perhaps not coincidentally, they all either made drawings or wrote things down that I've framed. These are my proof that I was, as George Trow said to me one time, "rescued by my own actions and didn't get killed."

THE ORIGINAL MARRIED MAN

I'll never be anywhere I like better than the veranda off my childhood bedroom in Palo Alto, California. My room was upstairs, fairly large, with a few French windows overlooking the garden. The bedspreads on my twin beds were quilted in cream-colored chintz with little claret-red rosebuds all over, the same as the curtains on the windows. From the ceiling hung a small chandelier with grapes on it, a friendly presence at night. But the thing that mattered most was the veranda. All the wisteria and magenta bougainvillea grew up onto the veranda, and when I lay there under the green awning on my collapsible chaise with green cushions, anything bad or ugly was automatically blacked out: gone.

The house in Palo Alto was made out of sandy-colored stucco, with cream-colored wood trim. Mother's mother and stepfather had built it in 1928. It had a pitched roof with a dark-green front door and a wrought-iron grille over a small window, and all the shutters were painted British racing green. I don't think of the house without seeing fairly bright, unde-pressing small green leaves all over it, but it didn't look as cheerful in winter, when the leaves fell off. Facing the street was an enormous blue spruce and two deodar cedars, the kind whose tops tip over. There was another hovering blue spruce (looking old, like the other, because the needles were silver), and a little boxwood hedge going all the way around the house. From the front door to the sidewalk was a winding brick path with violas (blue, lavender, white) on either side and, along the front sidewalk in the spring, purple iris, which looked too thin and unprotected against the street. They died fast.

Out in the back of the house, in a corner, stood a huge evergreen tree that could have been in Yosemite. A white owl used to sit in it. Across from a brick terrace, sort of in a row, stood some fruit trees: nectarine, apricot, peach, a flowering Japanese plum. Down in the garden were lilacs, daphnes, dahlias, and sweet peas, and cannas: big white flowers with orange centers. A stone wall went around the back of the garden and along one side of it. The grass out back was scalloped with tuberous begonias (the small ones) in a border. Outside the breakfast room were an orange tree and a grapefruit tree, but the fruit didn't grow very well: undersized, not so sweet, too pale. Not enough sun.

I never did think of myself as a person who would get married and live in a house. My mother and father seemed like two separate entities in our house, so to me marriage was a state and a house was a place where people who are wittily mean to each other live in an isolated way.

At the dinner table, my sister—she's six years older—and I would sit at our places in our school uniforms, navy pleated skirts and white middy blouses. A little crystal bell sat on the table by my mother's place, to call Nita, the maid. ("Don't forget the finger bowls and the butter balls," my sister told me on the telephone the other day.)

My father sat at the head of the table, in a chair with arms. The rest of us sat in chairs with no arms, but all of them, like his, were upholstered in dark yellow-gold damask. Oddly, there was a portrait of me in a white dress on the dining-room wall behind him. Daddy nearly always looked as if he were on the verge of losing control in one violent way or another, as if he were going to laugh at us or swat us away in a fit of bad temper. He had green eyes, a good color, but they often took on a sneering and impatient cast. His hair was very dark and straight, with some hair tonic in it. He usually wore a dark suit and a white shirt. In between courses, my father would rant about his patients (he was a psychiatrist) or his hatred of Communism, and my sister would be mute when he asked her questions about current world crises. Any answer she came up with to any question he asked was invariably wrong. My sister might start to cry, Mother saying, "Milton! You don't *hear* yourself," as he hollered some more. Other times my sister or I, or even my mother, would get up and run.

Because I never said a word at the table, he would sometimes turn his attention to me and say in a very loud voice, "How are you, Personality Minus?"—he had a way with language—or he yelled and threatened to send me to Agnew State mental hospital, near San Jose, where he frequently went on his after-dinner rounds. At other times, as if there were only the two options, he might say to me, "You're going to be a femme fatale, Babs." My mother and my sister and I were Babs I, Babs II, and Babs III to him, though none of our names resembled the name Barbara.

Nita, meanwhile, just kept coming in and out of the swinging door to the kitchen, punctuating my father's monologues with interludes of clattering dishes. Nita—her real name was Juanita Johnson—was a dark-chocolate black woman in a starched white uniform who had turned up in our kitchen in Palo Alto, thick glasses shielding a crossed eye, pomade stuff combed into her hair. We'd always had Japanese maids before. (There was an upstairs maid and a downstairs maid. "That's how people lived then, honey," Mother says now.) Nita said "uh-huh" continually, as if agreeing with what she'd just said. Even my father became subdued as she passed the food around in all those silver things.

The first night Nita served dinner at our house, my blond friend Squirrel was there—we were about twelve—and we giggled at Nita, because she didn't know about serving: she didn't know how to set a dinner table, didn't know where the dishes went, or how to clear the dinner plates: she stacked them one on top of the other, right at the table, food still on them.

My father, who was very tall and handsome, sometimes told witty, mean stories about his patients: a middle-aged woman, for instance, was frightened to put on a dress, a sweater, anything, over her head, "for fear she'd be stuck in the dark," he said, smirking. He wouldn't tell us a single thing about Doris Day, however, though she had been a patient of his. One youngish man was upset because his father owned a funeral parlor on the wrong side of town. There was the man who had to do everything twice: wash his face twice, brush his teeth twice, comb his hair twice, put on his clothes twice. The human race was really hopeless, according to Daddy. *He* got depressed by the patients—he said so. One time, he said all the homosexuals should be thrown in the Pacific Ocean. Too often he told scary, world-coming-to-an-end stories about his friend Robert Oppenheimer and his recent invention the atomic bomb.

Perhaps to cheer himself up, at breakfast he sang songs to himself like "I don't want her, you can have her, she's too fat for me" while Nita served him a soft-boiled egg and her shoulders shook with laughter. In his droll mode, he used to sing around the house, "It's great to get up in the *morn*ing, it's great to get up in the *morn*ing, it's great to get up in the mor*n*ing, but it's nicer to stay in bed." But he was in another mood altogether when he banged on my bedroom door. He would bang with both fists so hard it sounded as if the door would fall down, but it didn't. He would yell, each word dragged out unnaturally—he sounded literally brutal—*"Get . . . up . . . Babs!"* Then I would get up, put on my school uniform, and go downstairs to the breakfast room, where my father would say, from inside his perfect white shirt and his dark suit, *"Good morning, Babs!"*—loud. I never said "Good morning" back to him, and in fact I have never been able to say "Good morning" to anyone since. The worst banging on my door was during my sacred weekly ritual of watching Gardner McKay in *Adventures in Paradise,* one night a week. I counted on Gardner McKay to save me and he did. No matter how hard my father banged on the door, I knew Gardner McKay understood everything. The close-to-unnatural beauty of Gardner McKay's whole self, combined with a mixed-up-and-lost thing on his face, made me certain of that. No matter what, he was my weekly savior, complete with a vase of hand-picked flowers on top of the TV set, my bedroom door locked.

Most of my mother's friends (except the one who had been married to Otto Rank) had little crushes on my father. For Christmas, he got dozens of presents from those people whom Mother called "grateful patients."

Mother didn't know what to do with all the dinnertime violence. She seemed removed somehow from the chaos around her, an outsider, and would sometimes say, "I'm the only sane one around here!," as if she were defining a malady that separated her from the rest of us. Mother wore Chinese silk pajamas with a matching silk coat nearly every night. When she was twenty-one, Mother had been the only girl in a class at Yale Graduate School studying Chinese history. She told me this, or something like this, twenty million times, holding forth less on the history of peasant uprisings in twelfth-century China, or whatever, than on her professor—who had studied under So-and-So, and who often invited her to his house for a glass of sherry. Her mother had been brought up by Chinese servants, who gave her wedding presents—that's what servants did then—so those gifts were around the house, too: Chinese porcelain vases, bronze things.

My father believed that chemicals were the only way to make a mentally disturbed person reasonably sane. Like many people who believe things ahead of their time, he had a contract to write a book about it all but never finished it. My mother said that he hadn't wanted to have children, because he believed mental illness was hereditary and he didn't want them to suffer what he had suffered. She thought he tried out on himself the pills that he believed were going to work, to see what the effect was. This may have accounted for some of his more spectacular moods.

My friend Squirrel spent the night in my room often, her blond hair on the pillow on the other twin bed. This was the first time I had seen blond hair that early in the morning, and it seemed optimistic. Squirrel played Chopin on the big piano downstairs, and Schubert. I would make her play a Liszt rhapsody as loud and as fast as she could, faster and faster, and it was a kind of ecstasy to sit next to her on the black piano bench when she played.

Before Squirrel's arrival, I had three mops as best friends. This went on for two years when I was about ten and eleven. Most days after school, I'd take my mops dancing in the dahlia garden, where I had them all to myself. These were mops the maids used to clean the kitchen floor with. I would find them drying by the back door, between the garbage cans and the wooden milk box for the milkman. My mops were blond, like the blond girls at school who were older and taller than I was. I loved the mops' hair, soft yellowy-white rope, shoulder-length, which looked good wet, too—so thick!—and I loved the way it fell across their faces. Each mop's expression depended on how the soft rope had been horizontally stitched across her face. Their eyes seemed downcast. Since the stitching wasn't exactly the same, I could tell one face from the other, and one's hair was slightly shorter, or was parted in the middle, as opposed to a side part, or was lighter. I've always thought blond hair gives a color to the world that other hair doesn't. Blond hair gave a girl at school a different personality, different thoughts in her head, a fair entitlement. The bright-yellow tall, narrow bodies of my mops intensified their blondness. The way their hair smelled when it was semi-wet, maybe with a touch of kitchen bleach— that was nice, too. The mops were good dancers on the lawn, their rope-hair swaying this way and that, the way the grownup girls' did in my sister's fashion magazines.

My first love, though, had been my pencil collection. A few school years before, I'd had twenty-five pencils, mostly regular yellow ones: black lettering, black numbers, bands of black-and-gold metal at the end, worn-down pink erasers. There was one black pencil, with an odd square eraser—she was probably Jewish. They were a whole school of private friends, all girls, just the way it was at my real school. Their faces were that pencil-pale wood and smooth lead; I had to be careful with their faces. Each pencil had a first name, and most of them had last names, too, and every single one of them had a particular face. The shape of the face depended on how the pencil had been sharpened, how much lead there was above the wood, how rounded off the point of the lead was. Some of the pencils didn't get along with the others, but all of them were reliably faithful to and quiet with me.

One afternoon, my mother sharpened my pencils. Their faces were obliterated and unrecognizable. Some of them were a lot shorter, too. It was as if everyone I knew had a different head and face on a now stunted body. I couldn't look at them anymore, all distorted like that, so I abandoned them. In the years that followed, I would see one of the pencils around the house, by a telephone, vaguely recognizable, but dead.

There was a total education right there in our house, if anybody wanted it. Largely, this education consisted of men—older ones and, later, young ones—and books. Sometimes the men and the books collided. At first, caught up, as I was, in my pencils and mops, I didn't know I wanted this education. Daddy had said it didn't matter if I ever went to college. He said, "It doesn't matter if you ever do anything, Babs." An early boyfriend of my sister's pointed out Kafka, which was exceedingly helpful. There was the story about the man who lived by himself and thought about getting a dog because he was lonesome, but first he figured out the many reasons not to get a dog. Then some bouncing balls appeared in his apartment, following him around and bouncing underneath his bed all night, keeping him awake, until he thought of some scheme to control the bouncing. In the morning, the balls started bouncing again. Kafka made the floor feel like something to stand on, not slanted.

I talked about what I'd read to my father's friends. I did well with them. They were these big genius types, who came to dinner, or to visit. The shiest one was Bob Hofstadter, who won the Nobel Prize in Physics one year. He didn't talk much, but called often, saying, in a babyish voice, "Is Milton there?," as if it were embarrassing to ask, and he never identified himself. Haakon Chevalier, a close friend of Robert Oppenheimer's and an interpreter at the Nuremberg trials, was an old family friend, until one night at dinner in 1961 when he was eloquent in his praise of Communism. My father stood up from the table, went into one of his most violent rages, and, according to Chevalier's daughter, Suzanne, who was present, yelled, "Get the hell out of this house!" My father "threw Chevalier out," is how my mother puts it. The two men never spoke again. Daddy said that John Reed, who was teaching philosophy at Stanford, was a "genius, definitely," but Mother said he was a "genius who fizzled out." As to genius, Mother and Daddy also argued about Bertrand Russell, whom my father had known a little in Philadelphia in the forties.

John Reed was weighted down with sarcasm, abstraction, a bullying masculinity, and heartiness, and he talked with me about Kafka's bouncing balls. I don't think I understood what he said especially—I was eleven or twelve—but I did get that he was immensely funny about them. John Reed had to have everyone admire him, so that is what I did when he came over and talked about the absurdity of things. He had a sturdy type of body, a mustache, and a gruffness. He laughed using a lot of breath, as if huffing and puffing any bad thoughts away from him. It amuses me to think he's been dead for a while and that the preadolescent girl who sat across from him at dinner in Palo Alto is thinking about him, admiring him right now.

I started to have grownup boyfriends when I was about nine or ten. They were my sister's boyfriends, so in a way they were like married men—married to her. They went to Stanford (Daddy had been a freshman there when he was fifteen) and were "wishy"—a word I invented later, which meant "to be wished for." They came over to see me even if my sister wasn't there. They came over also because there was lots of food and the garden looked good. In late spring, after school, I'd put on a black nylon one-piece bathing suit and we'd lie by the pool, off the terrace, not far from the row of fruit trees, listening to Ella Fitzgerald sing, "Ten cents a dance, that's what they pay me, gosh how they weigh me down," which would be blasting from my father's phonograph, the living-room doors wide open.

I liked George Koenig the best of them all. There's a possibility I never liked any man better than George Koenig. "Gee, Ali, what's going on?" he would say, and listen to me talk about what had happened to the pencils lately, or about who I hated and why.

George was good-looking in a German, square-faced way, with sunken blue lugubrious eyes, dark lids, light-brown hair, not blond, parted on the side but disheveled. His whole self was the way Squirrel's blond hair had been when I first saw it, that bright and optimistic presence. Often he arrived in bicycle clothes—tight-fitting black shorts that stopped right below the knee and one of those striped Italian T-shirts. In 1960, he lost out on being in the Olympics by only half a wheel. Though my sister and George were spending a lot of time together in the downstairs bedroom (she was fifteen, sixteen already, he lived at the other end of the block and would climb in her window at night), he was always telling her how beautiful I was and that I was very smart. Making her feel stupid, just the way Daddy did. Like Daddy, too, George made fun of everyone and everything, but he was on my side instead of being an opponent. His laugh made even the dining room of the house unscary.

Or, he and my sister might be sitting in the living room, and I'd wander in, sit on the arm of their sofa, the upholstery unraveling from the cat's claws, my legs dangling (I wore shorts a lot), and George would say, "Doesn't Ali have great legs?" My sister wouldn't say a thing, or else she'd walk out of the room. It was the first time I understood the victory of cahoots-style cruelty (it's not lonesome for the two people who gang up on the other person), also of high-level, inventive flirtation. I learned how to use charm-or-whatever-it-was as if it were a passport. I didn't know where I thought I was going with this, but it never occurred to me to stop.

I thought George would always be there somewhere, but when I was fourteen he got married, in the Woodside Chapel, fifteen minutes from Palo Alto. About thirteen years later, under a completely blue sky at Lake Tahoe, where he was living with his second wife in a house he built himself, he showed me an old black-and-white photograph with wavy edges from that wedding day in 1958: me in a regular dress, my face all distorted from non-stop uncontrollable crying.

When George was gone, I lost what I'd wanted from him: constant, reliable protection. I'd known how to get it, but didn't have it now, and even though he visited me at the Annie Wright Seminary, in Tacoma, Washington, and wrote me letters there, he would visit with his wife, and I felt his irrevocable absence.

It isn't that I remember one particular day at the beach or something (we didn't *do* things, in the beachgoing sense). Three or four times, though, George Koenig had taken me for a ride in his maroon 1951 two-door coupe—a boxy-looking Ford—just around the Stanford campus, past the palm trees, Hoover Tower, everything Spanish, eucalyptus trees and oak, and I felt like an actual person. He would tell me I was smart and pretty and be droll about it, too—I guess because it was a peculiar sort of conspiracy: him eighteen, me ten. One afternoon, we actually drove thirty-five minutes to the top of Skyline Boulevard in Woodside, got out of the car, and stood there together. We had the whole run of the landscape. He had wanted, he told me after we'd grown up, to show me what it was like from above because I rarely left my room. Long before that day, he and I had started calling all the people down below—the enemy people, the ones who didn't see things our way, the ones who didn't get The Point, the whole Bay Area— the Grocery People.

Mother was attracted to George, you could tell by her whole demeanor: the way she adjusted her clothes, her jewelry; she was livelier in his presence. She kept all of George's favorite foods on hand for him—green apples, La Vache Qui Rit cheese, pastries from the bakery—or she'd rush out in her red Thunderbird and get them. She flirted with him. When George was with me alone at our house, Not Believing in Anything at All—as we called it—felt like a triumph, but when George was at our house and Mother would join us, being not droll but witty, it turned into a private attack of nothingness disease. To me, George talked about sinking into depression and laughed at the same time: he made the sinking seem alluring, kindred. Mother made it seem like a crime. Attachment to George Koenig, my consciousness of it, altered the depressive air in our household, and when he wasn't there with his derisive laugh I stayed in my room and played happily with my pencils or my animals. Perhaps he even taught me how not to miss anybody.

Last summer, almost half a century later, George Koenig and I did go to the beach, in Santa Cruz, after cocktails with Mother in the garden of her house in Atherton. In the car, I asked him why my father had threatened to send me to Agnew.

"Well," George said, taking me as seriously as ever, "that was the family business. That's like saying, 'I'm going to take the car in and have it fixed,' if you're a mechanic."

.   .   .

Sometimes the most fun person in the whole world to laugh with, to lose control laughing with, to laugh to the point where all else is obliterated, leaving no residue, can be my sister, Belinda. The place where we have done this laughing is in Mother's house in Atherton (Daddy died in 1983). In actual life elsewhere, and often there, we don't think the same things are funny, but when—only once or twice a year—we talk about Mother and Daddy and what it was like at home when we were young, we laugh so much we nearly cease to be human, just shaking, crumpled-up laughter with skin and clothes over it. There is often a sense of nausea before the laughing stops. It takes some time to recover. It's the only thing we have ever done that has made us feel inseparable, insofar as that blood thing people talk about.

Belinda has always got it exactly right about what Mother and Daddy wore and what the house in Palo Alto looked like. In this Atherton house, sitting at the dining-room table looking out through glass at a lot of grass, a giant oak tree, a fat palm off to one side—if you stand up, you can see the orchard, but that only looks good in summer—my sister says, of Mother, "Even on days she isn't seeing anyone, she always has her jewelry on. She's always ready to be 'Miss Jones, I presume.'" That's what Mother used to say when she opened her front door and found one or the other of us standing there. It's meant to be a brightly fake formality, but the truth is it makes us feel stupid on the doorstep, as if she really doesn't know who we are. "She does it in the *wrong context*," my sister says. I've always thought Miss Jones must be someone better than we are, maybe from England. I mean, there's no way to *be* Miss Jones, or be dressed like her, or have her education, or the accent. So my sister and I have hysterics. "She started doing it when I began to bring boys home," Belinda says.

"Everything she says is a saying," Belinda goes on. "Everything she says she's said before. She says everything she says to be witty. Other people thought it was funny. We didn't think it was funny. She talks right through you. She answers you before she knows what you're saying.

"They had cocktails in the living room before dinner. For the barbecues, she had those fabulous sundresses—those prints and the black one with the crisscross straps in the back, forties-like? I'll tell you one thing, the boys thought she was sexy, and she was. I was jealous." Belinda means her boyfriends, who came to barbecues every Sunday night while my father, still dressed in his suit and tie, tortured a huge piece of steak over the fire, an ironic attempt at playing father in suburbia.

The clothes and the things make up my sister's memory; otherwise she doesn't have much of a growing-up memory. She'll admit to that anytime. Belinda says the only thing she remembers is milk wagons with horses. "I have no childhood memories except that one, because it was a horse. In Philadelphia." (My parents lived in Philadelphia when Belinda was small.) But she remembers clothes. "Mother always wears gloves," my sister says. "She has at least a hundred or more pairs." There are long, narrow drawers full of kid gloves in Mother's bedroom, in the neatest piles. They might be important to her, those gloves. Before she goes out, when she opens the drawer to put some on, she'll talk about a pair she bought in Paris in nineteen fifty-something and a whole long story goes with it, generally a good one—the hottest psychiatric gossip of the time—about Otto Rank, and Anaïs Nin, and what mother's friend Estelle, who'd been married to Rank, had to say about them. Estelle was infuriated that Nin had established herself in the world as Rank's "associate"—"when she wasn't clinically trained at all," Mother will say. She'll talk fast, excitedly, as she says this, as if the whole thing had taken place five minutes ago.

"She has *all* the bed jackets and peignoirs," my sister goes on. "She always bought those things for herself. They were always pink or white or écru. She doesn't like blue. She *always* looked glamorous. I see what these women wear to bed in the movies and it makes me sick." Belinda both laughs and doesn't when she talks about Mother. "And remember the little fat mules? They had satin rope that looked like a pom-pom, and open toes and a heel that clicked when she walked. She wore those at night. Her toenails were always polished."

Mother had a little room with a dressing table whose skirt

was pink-flowered gray chintz with cerise piping. The bedspread and chaise longue in her bedroom were like that, too.
One day after school—I was eight, wearing my blue-and-white
checked school jumper—I told Mother I couldn't figure out if I
was a living thing or not, or real, or what the world was, or
where it started or ended, or what the sky was. I'd been having
these thoughts in bed at night; I thought I would die from
them. So I went to talk to Mother in her dressing room—the
only time I ever did that—and told her. I believed she would
know what to do about them. She was sitting at the dressing
table in a brown gabardine suit, waves on one side of her hair;
maybe looking for an earring. I wasn't sure whether she'd heard
me. After barely a moment, though, as if thoughtfully, she said,
"Well, maybe you can be put to sleep for a while. They put animals to sleep."

"Remember when the man came over with the gun—that
patient?" I say to Belinda. One morning when I was eight,
Daddy, over his English muffin at breakfast, told me that the
man who'd come by the night before—who'd looked just like a
regular man to me—had had a pistol on him.

"*No,*" my sister says, and changes the subject. Her face looks
more focused and more engaged when she talks about our
father. She's never considered him as droll a subject—as perversely charming—as I've thought he was, even though he
frightened me. "Women liked him. I never understood that,"
my sister said once, emphatically. "If I heard Mother talk about
one more degree of his from Yale, Brown, Stanford, Harvard, et
cetera, I was going to go through my skull. That's why I never
did anything." My sister was married for twenty years; she
doesn't mean she never did *anything*. She auditioned for the Bal-

lets Russes de Monte Carlo in San Francisco when she was thirteen, dancing for the prima ballerina, Alexandra Danilova. ("They were interested," she has said, "but I got such a case of the jitters that I ran right out of the rehearsal room, fast. I was so nervous I never could have gone to Russia or wherever you had to go. I never could have done that.")

She pauses now, then says, reciting, "He never went to war. He was 'Director of Public Health through the Red Cross for the Western United States'—I think that's how you say that. He started the Department of Public Health at U.C. Berkeley. Our grandmother rolled bandages in the First World War. I think he was the first psychiatrist in Palo Alto."

My sister has a tendency to rhapsodize about Daddy: "He was very kind to people. He saved a lot of people's lives. I heard that over and over and over again. Mother has coffee still with a woman whose life was saved by him." Girls at school used to say that to me, too. Everyone was always saying, "He saved my life," "He saved my mother's life," and all that, and just about everywhere: salespeople, doctors, even a ticket-taker in a movie theatre on the El Camino.

For a stretch of about five years when my sister was near and into adolescence and I was little, Mary Ann turned up at our house in Palo Alto. She was my father's secretary and research assistant. She'd graduated from Stanford, and helped him write papers; my father and she had some psychiatric program for children going on in the back of his office, a small one-story house on Forest Avenue. But what I remember is her being around our house a lot. She was just sort of always around. Everybody said she was very intelligent, a genius. When my parents were away, in Europe or somewhere, she would pick me up from dancing school—white cotton gloves, the fox-trot—on Friday nights. Sometimes, as a special treat, Mary Ann and I went, with my dog, Bambi, to the drive-in movies somewhere up the El Camino. Belinda was probably out on a date. I liked being in the car with Mary Ann.

Mary Ann was the only person in our house who didn't have fits of uncontrol; she never shouted, never showed if she was upset. It felt normal to have her there, though in fact being so self-possessed made her a freak in our house. Belinda in high school had all kinds of adolescent suspicions about Mary Ann being so normal, but I in grade school couldn't have cared less.

One time in some lodge in Carmel, I went into Mary Ann's room in the early morning—I was five or six—got into her bed, went down to the bottom of it, crawled back up out of the covers, and explained to her that I had just come out of her body, had just been born. She was nice about it, I remember. That's what I cared about.

"Did Mary Ann look good?" I ask Belinda.

"Mary Ann was tall—compact body," Belinda says. "Blue eyes, brown hair behind her ears, with combs—curly hair. She wore standard glasses with plastic rims. She wore a raincoat with a belt, sweater sets, and a straight skirt and nylons. She had sensible shoes and also had a handbag, as I recall. She was academic." On my last visit to Atherton, when Belinda and I were sitting in the breakfast room at the French table, with our croissants and jams and espresso and everything, and talking about Mary Ann, Mother came into the room. One of the things she'd always done was stand outside and eavesdrop and then butt in, walk into a room as if she'd been part of the conversation. Belinda was saying, "Mary Ann always said Mother didn't understand Daddy," when Mother came in, wearing one of her outfits with high heels, and said, "That wasn't true and I want it on my tombstone." Then she went clickety-clack into her study and shut the door, to make an important call to Washington or Paris.

My mother and father did do some nice things for me: Mother gave me a thirty-six-inch Steiff chimpanzee one Christmas. Another Christmas, she gave me a tall (nearly as tall as I was) rag doll with yellow, thick yarn for hair, a contented expression, and a blue dress. She took me to Carmel, to our house on the beach, and made me my first tuna-fish sandwich on white bread with mayonnaise and let me walk all the way down to the end of the beach to eat it by myself. She cooked me shells on Sunday nights (the servants were off on Sundays), with butter and hot milk, after I'd been horseback riding. She ordered pastel ice-cream animals for birthdays, though I got upset when they melted. She took me to San Francisco to buy dresses and coats at I. Magnin, and to Blum's afterward, for chocolate-fudge layer cake and cinnamon candies to take home. She drove me in her car to pick out Amber, a little blond cat (all mine), from a litter of kittens. She took me out in a rowboat on Lake Tahoe and taught me how to use the oars. When I was sixteen, she taught me to drink coffee before taking tests and writing papers, while staying up late, when I'd been feeling inadequate about schoolwork. Mother said coffee helped. She changed my life in this way.

Daddy would snicker with me, and laughed with me behind Mother's back when she talked to the maids; he gave me credit for quickness in idiocy detection. Mother couldn't hear us with the kitchen door shut, but, even if she had, she would have defended herself, confirming that we were lunatics, and rude, and that if we wanted to eat dinner we could plan it and cook it ourselves, or leave home, something like that.

The meanest we ever got, though—so thrilling—was in the hallway outside the kitchen when Mother and my sister would talk in infinitesimal detail about food. They talked about what food we'd had yesterday and compare it to other food. They talked about the food they were preparing to eat today and in the future, and it was as if they had a private language. The meanest part was that when the kitchen door was open they could hear us laughing. In the hallway, I would say, "Daddy, I can't take it." What he would say was *"Babsy Babs,"* loud but full of ironic intent, or else he'd say, a lot louder, *"Non*sense," which was an evaluation of Mother, my sister, and the whole wide world. And then he'd walk down the hallway toward his room so he wouldn't get caught.

Around the house, to himself he would say "Higgy Diggy Dig" to no one in particular and then laugh. None of us asked him what Higgy Diggy Dig meant; it was just something Daddy said. My father gave me Nonsense-at-Large as another passport to carry with me for life. I would not have survived knowing anyone, or doing anything, without it.

My father also, withholding almost all his irony, played catch with a ball on the back lawn with me when I was in grade school. This was his attempt at being outdoorsy. There were no words, and so no hollering. And yet, when I was five and fell on the carpeted stairs in our house and couldn't move (I was paralyzed for a week or so), he was his other, usual cold and weird self. He and Mother called the pediatrician, who arrived with his black bag, and they all stood over me and agreed it was an emotional disorder, not polio.

Sometimes, however, after a calm dinner, when I was older and in school, Daddy took me in his black Mercedes on his after-dinner rounds, up to Sequoia Hospital, in Redwood City, which was a normal hospital with a mental ward in it. He never took me to visit Agnew State, because it was an asylum. As he drove, he would talk—in an even-tempered, informative voice—about things in the newspaper, things in the world. Just after my mother's mother died, he took himself on a trip to India, and afterward would tell me in some detail about the dead dogs all over the streets of Bombay, calling it "the dead-dog city." Other times he continued his dinner-table rants on Russia or the A-bomb or President Eisenhower, even-tempered this time.

We drove up the El Camino, past the cheap motels, a drive-in restaurant, and an animal hospital, where I imagined all the animals dying next to one another in cages. Leaning into the steering wheel in his black car, polished shoe on the gas pedal, he looked more devil-may-care than he did with his semi-permanent scowl inside our house. In the car, he looked as if he were laughing to himself, though he didn't laugh, and he drove fast, as if all the cars and headlights on the highway should get out of his way. I didn't say anything, but the occasional "How are you, Babs III?" didn't require an answer. I thought these trips were an exclusive little excursion to where "crazy" literally was—not "going crazy" but going to an actual physical place.

Inside the hospital, I'd wait for him in the white reception area—sit on a chair and do nothing—while he disappeared down a long corridor and through some doors. Mother often said I was better at doing nothing than anyone she'd ever met. He was in there for an hour or so, most times. On the way in or the way out, my father might introduce me to someone. "Dr.

Adler, this is my daughter Alison," a wry lilt in his inflection. He seemed to like to show me off, say the word "daughter," use my real name. There was an extraordinary giddy quality to these outings, much like my car trips with George Koenig.

These car trips with my father always began in the same way. Daddy would get up from his armchair in the living room, where he and my mother were having demitasse, and laugh out loud to himself. Then he would say, as if it were the greatest fun a father and daughter could have together, "Come on, Babs III!" I'd get a little overcome to be so singled out; Mother and my sister didn't get invited to the mental ward. I was the one, and in this way Daddy gave me style. He wrote my character.

I was alone with my father one afternoon, a rarity outside of his driving me to school or to visit the mental ward. I was eleven. We were walking above the beach at Carmel, along rocks and some shore grass. I felt proud to be with him. He seemed extra-tall, and wore a navy cardigan sweater, on a separate plane from other people, and then he ruined the conspiracy when he pointed to a young man and woman and a baby who were on the wet sand, close to the smallest waves, and as I looked at them he said, *"That's the point, Babs!"* He said it very loud. He said it *very* loud, maybe louder because we were outside, his manner stern. He said it as if, had there been any chance I would come up with another reason to live, I'd be dead wrong. This was a contradiction to everything else he ever said about humans. Maybe in that way, too, he wrote my character.

He was a bully and a tyrant and some kind of handsome star and completely depressed and droll. It stands to some kind of reason, then, that I might think a perfect boyfriend was a bully and a tyrant and some kind of handsome star and completely depressed and droll. Harold Brodkey, as things turned out later, was exactly like that, *exactly,* and so were Billy the Fish and George Trow, although they were shorter, possibly bossier, and blond.

PLAY HOUSE, MES ENFANTS

Francine and I sublet a ground-floor apartment at 300 Central Park West in New York City. Francine made the living room—dark furniture, heavy drapes—her territory. She had trunks of clothes all over the place which her mother sent to her. Francine—she's from Atlanta—was so unnervingly beautiful that ugliness of all sorts fell to pieces wherever she was. It was as if someone had made her up, out of longing. Francine was so pretty that people felt disoriented around her. She wasn't like a regular human girl. You could feel her spirit, and her startling kindness. She said to me, several times, "You're so pretty—your hair's like mink." She had a long, straight, Grecian nose—no one I'd ever seen had a profile like hers—and I remember thinking that her eyes, almost dark blue, looked like Montgomery Clift's. They opened and closed slowly as she talked. She had thin, muscular, ballerina upper arms and a large doll's head and face, like a nineteen-thirties screen idol. She had no hips at all.

The first time I ever saw her, in the fall of 1964, or a few months before, was in one of the dingy little white rooms in the

Barbizon Hotel for Women, on Lexington. At the Barbizon, men were allowed in the lobby and in the dining room, but never upstairs. The elevator ladies wore belted brown uniforms, like guards in nineteen-forties movies. For generations, mothers had sent their daughters there, so they would be safe from men. One of Francine's aunts had been a roommate of Grace Kelly's at the Barbizon twenty-five years before. Francine's aunt had told her that Grace Kelly talked to herself in the mirror all the time.

The day I first met Francine, she was getting ready to go out on more than one date. She always had two or three dates planned for every evening. Men called and lined up and waited to get to see her whenever she could fit them into her night life. Suzy the columnist saw Francine at balls, and invited her to even more balls. As she got ready to go out, Francine sat cross-legged in a yellow Jean Harlow–type nightgown holding a large hand mirror and putting on Aziza cake mascara. It took her forty-five minutes. That evening, Francine was wearing a black crêpe just-below-the-knee sleeveless sheath, black sheer stockings, and black peau-de-soie high heels. Her blond hair was parted in the middle and pulled back into a chignon. She had definite muscles in her calves.

On the floor of her room at the Barbizon was an uneaten grilled-cheese-with-bacon sandwich, with a half-empty glass of iced tea, a gathering of makeup, and in the middle of the room a hanging-rack jammed with black cocktail dresses—they rustled when she brushed against them—and other clothes. Francine said I could wear any of those dresses if I wanted to. Once, when I borrowed a wool coat with a gray fox collar, she said, "The way your hair is resting on the fur is just perfect." Conversation with Francine was a little out of sync, because her spirit moved at its own pace. There wasn't any sarcasm or hostility in the air around her. However she did it, Francine's beauty made me feel protected, calm. She was so nice there wasn't anything else to do except let any envious thought in my head go completely away, at least until she'd put on a little black coat and white gloves, and left to go out on her dates.

Francine came from a dynasty of beauties. Her mother, Frances, was the oldest of five sisters—the others were Corinne, Evelyn, Maybell, and Marvine—from the hills of Tennessee. They looked different from what ordinarily passes as female in the human race; every one of them had made men's heads not only turn but swirl and go out of control. They all had variations of the same face Francine has, and thick blond hair. Except for Evelyn, who had red hair—"like Rita Hayworth's," Francine always said. When they were teen-agers during the Depression, the sisters had fights about which one was the prettiest, and Evelyn always won. They were all tall, too—five feet eight or nine—and had really small waists and no hips and long legs. Frances had the thickest natural platinum-blond hair. "Like Lana Turner's," Francine said. A governor of Georgia once referred to Francine's mother as the Eighth Wonder of the World. I met Francine's mother in the Regency Hotel on Park Avenue. Even in her early forties she was shockingly, glamorously beautiful. She was cold, though. Francine told me her mother looked in her bedroom mirror—it was ten feet tall and six feet wide—all the time. After she died, Francine put that mirror down in her basement.

During the Depression Francine's mother and sisters nearly starved to death. Their father was a bootlegger, and out of the picture. The sisters all slept in one big bed together and had to brush their teeth with twigs, because there weren't any toothbrushes. Frances had to clean toilets in the high school and work in a dime store to bring home money for their mother. All that time none of them were too upset, Francine told me, because they knew their beauty would get them out of the hills of Tennessee, as it did. Maybell met an admiral in the Navy, out West; Francine's mother married her high-school sweetheart and moved to Atlanta, where she divorced and remarried. The other sisters all moved to San Francisco and got married and divorced and married and divorced and married and divorced, drifting back and forth from San Francisco to New York. When Evelyn moved to New York the first time, Walter Winchell said about her, "The most beautiful woman in the world has come to New York." Evelyn often said that one day she was going to walk into the Pacific Ocean and never come back, and that's what she did, in Santa Monica. Police and detectives never found her, and she never washed ashore. Frances ended up rich from an interior-decorating business she started on her own after she remarried. She was so beautiful nobody could believe her décors wouldn't be.

At seven years old, Francine had flown from Atlanta to New York by herself. She was an only child and had been living with a grandparent. When she arrived at the airport, her mother and all of her aunts were standing by the gate, each holding a Madame Alexander doll. Francine's mother kept Francine in strict beauty training all her life. The regimen was severe, an imprisonment almost. Her mother didn't talk to her about anything else.

"Nothing is more important than how you look and how you dress," her mother repeated to her over and over again. She also said, "Use your wares. Show off your looks. Never go out without being fully dressed or without makeup." When Francine was about two and a half, she and her mother lived for a time in a hotel room in St. Louis. There was nothing to play with, so Francine made a slide out of the ironing board while her mother made beautiful cocktail dresses for herself out of black or brown silk taffeta, with big, full skirts. She had an eighteen-inch waist. When Johnnie Ray came on the radio singing that blues-tinged song about crying—a hit all over the world—Francine would dance to it. Frances would lay the fabric on the floor, cut it out, and, with a sewing machine, sew it all together.

Frances was so fair her eyelashes were white. When she was pregnant with Francine, Frances told her, she had rubbed her belly and prayed out loud: "Please let her have black eyelashes. Please let her have black eyelashes." Francine's eyelashes turned out to be dark brown, and for as long as I've known Francine it has taken her forty-five minutes to put on black mascara. I've timed it.

Francine's mother had more rules for beauty: Never let a drop of sun fall on your skin, nor one drop of water on your face (washing your face washes your skin away), never dye your hair, use an eyelash curler only when you're older. Always keep a lightweight scarf in your handbag. She had Francine wearing a girdle and a waist cincher when she was a teen-ager, even though Francine was really thin. Her view of mental health was similarly bracing. "You'd have to be out of your mind to give a psychiatrist money when you could go out and buy a new pair of shoes."

Whenever Francine's mother was in a fitting room in a department store trying on clothes, she would drape the light-weight scarf over her head and face, take the two back points, pull them forward, and tie them under her chin so she wouldn't ruin her lipstick or her hair. Saleswomen were astonished to find her in the fitting room with her head covered up.

When she was thirty, Francine fractured her nose—I've never noticed a flaw in her profile—and her mother said to the plastic surgeon, "It's better to leave it the way it is than to have a nose job, but she's ruined—it's just the end of her." Francine's mother had always thought that Francine was not entirely up to code. A favorite expression was "You can't make a silk purse out of a sow's ear," and another was "A man will walk a million miles for a good woman." Francine explained to me, "She meant not sleeping with anyone. You had to be a lady." Aside from striving to obey the rules of beauty, Francine had no identity whatsoever. "Thank God I didn't raise my children that way," she says now.

"I was the most charming little girl in the whole world," she adds, a bit ruefully. "I had perfect manners, I dressed perfectly. Mother said it would get me a rich husband, but I didn't want one." The swarms of men around Francine made her feel isolated. Though it was amusing to have them around, their obsequiousness toward her made them seem idiotic, so there were times when all Francine wanted to do was be alone. She didn't think there was anything wrong with a woman wanting to be alone.

Though of course it was impossible to live a normal life with people staring at her all the time, Francine had considerable fun being a beauty. Whenever she was living in New York, she went to countless formal balls, and was always out dancing at, as I remember it, Le Club and El Morocco (*the* night spots in New York in the sixties); the Maisonette, where Peter Duchin often thought she was Tuesday Weld; L'Interdit, where a man turned her around and forced her face to the light just so that he could see her eyes. She used to come back to the Barbizon and later to Central Park West to change her clothes for the night's second or third date. She lived in a world where she was rare, and she liked it. She says now, laughing, "I didn't have to look back and I didn't have to look forward. I loved being the center of attention on any dance floor. That's why I stayed up all night."

Nowadays, when we talk, she can't think of anyone she had a little crush on back then who didn't have a greater one on her. Even at the time it wasn't like any other girl's life I had ever heard of.

The story that Francine was really proud of was about the time that Charlie Chaplin watched her perform a ballet solo in the ballroom at the Palace Hotel in Montreux when she was eighteen and a half. When Francine was eighteen, her mother had bought her a lot of clothes and sent her to finishing school at La Châtelainie, in Gstaad. Francine had been in the Atlanta Ballet Company for five years, dancing every day, but they didn't teach ballet at La Châtelainie, and no student had ever had permission to leave the school to take classes elsewhere. One afternoon, when the owner of the school, Albert-Henri Jobin, was sitting outside the main chalet by himself, Francine almost crawled, she said, into Monsieur's lap and told him she couldn't live without ballet. M. Jobin knew she was telling the truth, and he found a ballet mistress who had danced with Pavlova's company and taught in a grand ballroom in Montreux. (One day around Christmastime, while about sixty girls were having lunch from silver trays, M. Jobin opened the door to the dining hall, surveyed the room, looked directly at Francine, and said, "Au revoir, mes enfants." Later that evening, he shot himself.) Every week Francine took an hour-and-a-half train ride through the mountains to Montreux for ballet lessons. At the Palace

Hotel, for a recital, there was a grand piano and a pianist on the ballroom stage. Francine wore a black tutu and black satin toe shoes, and she danced en pointe to "Sleeping Beauty." After the solo, at a little reception, Chaplin came up to her and said, "You were the best ballet dancer here today."

.   .   .

When we lived together on Central Park West, Francine was never afraid to leave the house. I, on the other hand, barely went outside. One night, though, on the way back from buying Betty Crocker brownie mix on Columbus, I actually *found* a beautiful young man, in front of our apartment, passed out drunk. I dragged him inside, which was hard, because he was six feet tall. His name turned out to be Duncan, and soon we were living in weird hotels together and both staying in all day, except for going down to the deli for bologna with green olives in it. Francine was off to Atlanta. I didn't have enough money to keep the apartment, so I gave it up.

Staying in hotel beds with cheesy sheets on them with Duncan all day was a whole life, as if there weren't a need to do anything else. In this way we were hating the world and reading Rimbaud as we hated: *A Season in Hell*—"*Je finis par trouver sacré le désordre de mon esprit.*" I was nineteen and he was twenty-six, so we didn't really know what weariness was. Our spirits' disorder, however, was sacred.

That summer was insufferably hot. At night we lived in bars until closing time: Sorabaja, on the Upper East Side; the White Horse, in the Village; Chumley's, where we would watch Zoot Sims put dimes in the jukebox. We'd stay until 4 a.m. and then go to our hotel, or, if neither one of us had the money, to some abandoned apartment house in Hell's Kitchen or somewhere, one that didn't have a front door on it, just an empty space. We used to have sex in places like that. There were other people there, too, not *right* there but maybe up a flight of stairs; I could hear them.

When we didn't have anywhere else at all to go, we'd spend the night in Central Park. We didn't have anything to sleep on, but the smell of the grass was nice, and he propped me up so that my head was on his chest. Sometimes my head slipped off and there was just the grass under my face, but we did stay there all night. One morning, a soldier in uniform was sleeping facedown on an old maroon blanket not that far from us. Duncan wondered if the soldier had a gun, but we didn't see one, and he didn't move when we got up to leave.

Francine was flying from Atlanta to New York, back and forth. In 1964, when Alfred Hitchcock was staying at the Atlanta Cabana Motor Hotel, just before *Marnie* opened, Francine's mother sent him two dozen yellow roses and called to make an appointment for Francine to meet him. She thought he might want to put Francine in the movies. When Francine arrived at his hotel room, it turned out that he had thought he was going to be interviewed by a journalist, and Francine had to explain: "No. My mother wanted me to meet you." He was very kind, sat in a big chair, and talked to her for hours. "He did all the talking," Francine said. He was "very polite, apologetic" when he said to her, "I just spent a million dollars on Tippi Hedren and I can't do that again right now."

At Christmas, Francine flew from New York to Las Vegas to see her mother and her Aunt Marvine, who was living there. She was waving goodbye out the airplane window to a boyfriend and so didn't see Eddie Fisher sit down in the seat next to her. Fisher was with his manager—they and Francine were the only people in first class. When Fisher said, "What are you doing?," Francine said, "I'm waving goodbye to my boyfriend and I'm going to Las Vegas to meet another one." She was wearing a brown sealskin coat with a mink collar, and Fisher said, "You should always wear fur." On the trip, he kept singing "Oh! My Papa" to her while she was trying to sleep.

"When Eddie Fisher and I got off the plane, Mother was there with Aunt Marvine trailing behind her," Francine said. "They looked so much alike. They were always dressed, always, and there was a big to-do over Mother wherever she went. If you got more than one of them together, there was a bigger to-do.

"We had to go to his show every night. He had us sitting right in the front. He'd dedicate a song to me and my mother, and we'd have to stand up." She laughed. "I just hate Las Vegas."

I always let Francine know which hotels Duncan and I were staying in—for a while, it was the Wellington, on Seventh Avenue and Fifty-fifth Street—and sometimes if she didn't feel like going home after her last date she would come find us there. Once, she settled in to spend the night with us, Duncan in the middle. At some time during the night, I had him move to my side of the bed—switch—so that I was in the middle. Lying there, I felt I had what people call a "family"—two humans of different sexes right up close. Real security and affection seemed to be a beautiful insane man by my side and my best blond girlfriend.

Like me, Duncan got some money from home—his came from North Carolina. Tennessee Williams called him a couple

of times, and with him Duncan's voice would get more Southern, would become a real drawl. I was jealous of Tennessee
Williams. In the beginning, I had little fantasies of marrying
Duncan. I pretty much gave up on that when I had to put him
in Gracie Square Hospital because he thought God was talking
to him in the Wellington Hotel. It seemed that I was develop-
ing a sort of ruthless, practical side. I was sad when I had Duncan committed; we had been like *Les Enfants Terribles* together.

Francine had moved back to New York again and rented a
studio on East Fifty-seventh Street. We lived there together
briefly. But when she went out to Los Angeles, because Gene
Kelly wanted her to audition to dance in a movie, I was by
myself there for only a week, because of Dill, a short gay man I
ended up calling Mother. He made me feel saved. This was in
1964, when I was nineteen.

I had met Dill—and he *was* salvation—in a photographer's studio on Seventeenth Street. I was more or less swirling against
gravity before I met Dill. I never knew what I was doing in
New York City, exactly, besides being away from California. A
photographer who worked for *Harper's Bazaar* had taken endless photographs of me and Duncan in Central Park. Some
of them were so good that this photographer said I should
take them to an agency, which I did, in an aggressive, close-to-
hallucinatory state of mind. Eventually, the agency—this is
what they normally do—sent me downtown to Seventeenth
Street, to be looked over for a magazine advertisement, I forget
which one, and the minute I met Dill we talked and talked: it
was that nothing-can-kill-it complicity you can find in combat
against what Philip Roth has called "the limitless Anti-You."
But the main attraction for me was Dill's trustworthiness. If I

was free to say nonsense out loud—to suddenly remark (though not on that first meeting), "Roasted and toasted!" or "Normal pie!"—Dill and I were connected, eternally. I never think I'm wrong about these things. And, besides, I'd had serious training from Daddy, the authority on nonsense. I was wearing a short white Mexican wedding dress (I'd been worried coming downtown that it would get dirty on the subway platform, or rushing into the car with all the people) and those white, stiff, short boots that were popular then, and black false eyelashes with whitish pale-pink lipstick. My hair was shoulder-length then, with heavy bangs that covered my eyebrows.

Dill was around five feet eight, with dark hair cut in a normal man's length for the mid-sixties, not short and not long. He had brown, almond-shaped eyes that looked as if he might lose all his self-discipline and laugh inappropriately, at any second, which he often did. He had an olive complexion, with some freckles if you looked closely. His nose was medium-length, an enviable nose, very straight in profile, and his lips were unexpectedly full. His body had a robotic stiffness, and his face never looked distorted, even though he was fundamentally "angry all the time," he says now. The day we met, he was wearing khaki trousers and a khaki jacket, like a uniform—in fact, he wore it daily for years. He had no interest in clothes. He liked taking photographs (still-lifes of eggs in an egg carton), reading Japanese writers, and listening to classical music. There was no one he held in higher esteem than Maria Callas, so on an irrational day of envy, all by myself in our apartment, I smashed one of his Maria Callas records to pieces with the handle of a big knife and Scotch-taped the pieces to the wall. When Dill came home from work and saw Maria Callas in fragments on the wall, he calmly removed them and put them in the garbage can. "That's too bad," he said in a robot voice. The incident was never mentioned again.

After the shoot on the day we met, he asked me out to dinner—it was the beginning of evening already—and we took the I.R.T. uptown, got some food somewhere, and then he came over to the studio on Fifty-seventh Street, slept in the other one of the twin beds Francine had bought, and stayed for the next five years. He made one trip to Brooklyn, where he had been living with his parents on Ocean Parkway, to pick up some clothes. He was thirty-three when he signed on to become Mother.

To me, a mother was a person who paid the rent and made certain the house ran properly, and shopped for groceries (Total cereal, kitty litter—Dill and I had a cat called Whipper that I bought on Lexington) and whatever else was necessary to keep existence going. I didn't care enough about existence to keep it going properly myself. Dill made me go to Alexander's with him to buy a vacuum cleaner—"You were very focused on being at home. I had to drag you out," he says now—and we made trips to E. J. Korvette's, a famous discount store on Fifth Avenue and Forty-seventh Street, for a tool kit and a record player for classical records that, when you bought them at Korvette's, cost ninety-nine cents. I still charged clothes at Bendel's and Bergdorf Goodman to my real mother, because that was the pact between her and me.

On Christmas and birthdays, she sent me a copy of a paid Bergdorf bill. The items I had charged were circled in red pencil. On the bill itself she had written, also in red, something along the lines of "I was going to send you the Croix de Guerre, but this and a little something from Procter & Gamble will have to do. Love, Mother."

I can still feel Mother's long-distance charge-account protection all around me when I am on the escalator at Bergdorf
Goodman. There is a note I kept from 1965. "I didn't receive a
bill from Bergdorf Goodman this month. I think that makes
me feel lonely." I wasn't lonely. On weekdays Dill took me out
for dinner every night, after he got home from work. Every
night I ordered half a roast spring chicken.

Dill took a lot of photographs of me. He was kind of
obsessed with taking pictures and he also did it for love of me.
He took one of my face for Clinique, but even when it was all
over one wall at Bloomingdale's and in Le Drugstore in Paris,
the very mention of it made me feel fat. An hour before the
shoot, I had eaten an amazing amount of Chinese food, and, all
by myself, an entire Sara Lee orange cake.

During this time, I savagely, perhaps foolishly, turned down
a proposal of marriage from someone I used to call Wheat
Field—a blond, aristocratic boy I'd known since I was seven,
who was leaving Harvard to live in Great Britain. A couple of
years ago, he said in a restaurant on Forty-third Street, "I quite
loved you when I was at Harvard." Somehow I couldn't feel that
a nice thing was happening to me, whatever I may think now,
and so I stayed on with Mother Dill.

It's possible to have fun with inappropriate behavior and doing
the wrong dance with the wrong people. With Baby Bob, say,
whom I'd known for a while now. I haven't met anyone since
who was in any way like him. Physically, he was a big, sweetly
distorted, pear-shaped human, as if not real somehow, maybe
blown up with air, or filled with gelatin. His feet didn't seem to
touch the ground; he might have been floating or rolling above
the ground, despite the heaviness. His thighs were a simple
drawing of capital "V"s. There was an odd, uncruel prettiness

in his face. Still, it didn't seem like a real boy's face. His mouth, which turned up at the corners but didn't close all the way, gave the impression he wasn't sad. An astonishment in his expression was partly that open mouth and, I decided, partly just a dumbfoundedness at being a living creature.

Baby Bob had turned up like this: One afternoon, I got a telephone call from a polite, bashful-sounding boy. He said a girl from Palo Alto had suggested he call me. In school, this blond girl had been one of the most authentically normal girls anybody could look for: athletic, smart, nice, pretty, president of the student body. This boy told me the girl had been a friend of his at Austen Riggs, a mental hospital in Stockbridge, Massachusetts (William Inge had got treatment there). She had told him to call me when he left. He invited me over to his apartment—his very first apartment, he said. It was a real invitation, for such-and-such a day, to come over for lunch. He warned me he was very fat.

Baby Bob's apartment was on West Seventy-sixth Street, between Central Park West and Columbus. I took a taxi over, rang the buzzer, walked up a flight or two, and there he was outside his apartment door, waiting to greet me. He was roly-poly round; he looked soft. He wasn't very tall, about five feet six, an inch taller than I. On that day, he weighed a hundred and eighty, he said—said it almost right away. Baby Bob had a tendency to get carried off into fits of unembarrassed high-pitched giggling, as if there were things in his mind that were so disturbing that hysterical giggling was the sole way to keep himself present in the conversation. It was great fun to join in. It was the beginning of spring when I went over to Baby Bob's apartment for lunch.

In the apartment, I confessed to Baby Bob that I felt a little fat, because I thought he would know everything about fatness.

I told him about fatness and ruination, about bookings for
Vogue and *Harper's Bazaar* that I would call and cancel because I
had eaten myself into an immobile, amorphous state that kept
me in bed recovering. On one occasion, however, in a pink
linen dress—I wasn't at all fat—I was sent to see Richard Avedon, who had his assistant book me: four editorial pages in
Vogue. This, I told Baby Bob, had included passing the inspec-
tion of Diana Vreeland, at Condé Nast, in the Graybar Building, next to Grand Central. I felt like a person walking over
there in that dress, not like an impostor, not altogether completely like an impostor.

A reprieve: that's what it was. Mrs. Vreeland, dressed in
black, had nodded with approval later as I stood on a platform
in front of a full-length mirror, in a black cocktail dress she'd
had me put on, like one Francine would wear. I don't think
Mrs. Vreeland said anything as she adjusted the dress on my
body with unstoppable authority. An assistant got down on the
floor and put pins in the dress. This time, though, I was pun-
ished not by me but, severely and perversely, by the nefarious
booking agent, who had reported (Avedon's empathetic assistant told me) that I would be out of town on the day of the
shoot.

The agency had been promoting another girl, I told Baby
Bob now. He didn't giggle. He seemed to know I wanted an
Avedon photograph—a great big black-and-white picture,
including my face—to prove I did exist, hadn't ended up in
Agnew State after all. George Trow, years later, understood the
phenomenon, too, knew all about it; "Darling, that's too bad,"
he said when I told him the same story. "When you're young
you can get away with a photograph. Now you have to write a
little poem just to keep up."

Baby Bob and I had sat down at a table near his kitchen—his studio apartment overlooked the street—and he made tuna melts in this cheap tin toaster oven his mother had given him. He silently empathized with my degradation, self-inflicted or otherwise. I sat there and pulled on my eyelashes.

Every so often during lunch he laughed his giggly, high-pitched hysterical laugh, a trail of giggles—they felt friendly—and I could hear the saliva hitting his teeth and see it spurting out in a little spray. At lunch I referred to the gray dress I had on as a "baby dress" and used the word "baby" as an adjective to describe lots of things: a baby dinner, a baby friend. And he began to do it. My friends used "baby" the way I did and that's how Bob got the name Baby Bob and I got called B'B'B, which is the way he writes it. Short for Baby Baby Baby.

The summer that I spent nights in the Park with Duncan, he and I would sometimes go in the mornings to Baby Bob's to sleep, forcing him out to spend the day at the Thalia, the revival house on Ninety-fifth off Broadway. Despite the heat, Bob wore the same pair of wool trousers every day; he was so fat he wouldn't buy any clothes. He pressed the wool trousers by putting them between the mattress and the box spring at night. Even though Bob minded being dislodged, he was polite about it, saying, as he retrieved the trousers and put them on, "You have to freshen up, you have to, for God's sake."

"I learned a whole way of relating to the world from you," Baby Bob said to me recently. He had only just moved to New York from Austen Riggs the spring we met, and knew even less than I did about getting by. I even taught him about the subway, he said. "If I hadn't met you I really would have died. I'd never been on my own before and *you were the only guide I had.*"

Baby Bob's tuna melts called for half a jar of mayonnaise, one can of tuna fish, eight slices of cheddar cheese, a slice of white bread for each of us. We were agitated waiting for the cheese to melt: it was as if there was nothing to do until the cheese melted, because all we wanted to do was eat the sandwiches—it was like waiting to inhale smoke when a cigarette's between your fingers and you can't find a match. Over the months, this agitated waiting for food became a big theme: what activities to undertake until whatever food we were preparing or buying was ready to eat. One day we actually made an assembly line of bacon-and-tomato sandwiches. We were eating sandwiches while toasting more bread, grilling more bacon, spooning mayonnaise, and slicing more tomatoes. I think we got through half a loaf of Wonder Bread.

We had quite an attachment to Sara Lee frozen cheesecake. We would go to D'Agostino's and buy three at a time. This way we had one cheesecake to eat on the way home, one to eat in the apartment while it was still frozen, and another to put in the refrigerator, the way they tell you to do it on the package, to defrost for two hours. Eating the one that was still frozen was something for us to do while the third Sara Lee reached its best consistency.

One night on our way home we passed the Copacabana nightclub. Glamorous young people were stepping out of taxis and greeting each other and wearing fur coats. They all seemed to be saying happily, "Hi, Charles!," and there Baby Bob and I were in our peacoats—we had twin peacoats—and with our brown paper bags of Sara Lee orange cake, our hands in the bags, the frosting stuck to our fingers.

When Baby Bob wasn't eating, he read everything, all of S. J. Perelman, and *In Cold Blood, Silent Spring, The Crack-Up*—we read aloud this part: "One should, for example, be able to see that things were hopeless and yet be determined to make them otherwise"—and he read Proust, all of it. I read *East of Eden,* allotting myself a particular number of Heinz sweet pickles per chapter. I wanted California—that Salinas and Monterey part—as close to me as I could get it, for solace. I sliced the pickles, to make them go farther.

Baby Bob and I went on other, slightly more legitimate diets together. One was a white diet. He charged a whole set of white dishes to his mother at Saks, "white china dishes that have never seen sugar or white flour"—the point was to start from scratch. We made an angel-food cake, but while waiting for the angel-food cake to bake we broke down and ate some M&Ms and wrecked the purity of the whole thing. We used to listen to the Time Lady on the phone to make sure we knew exactly what time to start our diets. For instance, a Fourth of July diet really had to begin precisely on the fourth. So we would call Time, and eat brownies until 11:59 p.m. on the third, and then stop eating. Otherwise the diet was ruined. We ruined our diets all the time.

Over the telephone the other day Baby Bob said, "People remember their graduations, weddings, first jobs. I just remember what I weighed on certain dates. I weighed a hundred and forty-five when John F. Kennedy was shot. I was thin for the blackout in 1965—I must have weighed a hundred and thirty for the blackout. I weighed a hundred and sixty-two when the men landed on the moon. But I was on my way down. With all the things that were going on in the world, nothing made an impact except the food. I judged the passage of time by that." Then he said, "When I first met you I was on my first fantastic diet, the one where I would lick Accent out of the palm of my hand before going to sleep. I remember having tea—and I *never* drink tea—in cafeterias around New York, waiting to lose another pound and to see you."

For about four years Dill and Baby Bob and I were a little odd-ball animal family for each other, reliable, with Dill as the single mother. My real mother said recently that Dill was "polite, like a devoted slave. I knew he was a homosexual but in those days we didn't talk about it. Nobody talked about it." She also said, "He was humble. No matter what happened to him, he kept doing his best." I didn't know it at the time, but Mother sent him checks once in a while, to cover some expense or another, so as it turns out she was the mother behind the mother, which made me a little sad when I found out, as if I had been betrayed by both mothers. By Dill because he hadn't been as stalwart and loyal as I had thought he'd been (it killed me that he'd talked about me behind my back), and by my own mother because she'd been interfering in our little sheltered oddball-animal-family life.

We never had a plan about anything. Our oddness got in the way of ordinary human connection with others. I have tended to stay in every one of my rooms, and especially when I had the apartment on Fifty-seventh Street I would limit my exposure to the outside world. Dill understood my resentment of human nakedness in summer. I didn't want to wear these new skimpy, short clothes that showed so much skin, right in front of strangers. Grim sidewalks and polished-stone storefronts didn't go with pale, sweating flesh; and glass just reflected more of it. So little privacy! My windows overlooked the Sutton Theatre, and I felt sorry for the people standing in the movie lines down there: older women with sagging skin and clammy upper arms, young women yanking down tiny skirts to cover their hind-quarters in the steamy air. I only wanted to stay inside.

ON THE LITTLE STAGE

To get my nerve up, I went to a phone booth in the Plaza Hotel to call Wynn Handman. Mother and I had stayed there when she brought me to New York the very first time, so in the Plaza I felt courageous and irrationally safe. Dill had been watching me fail to call Wynn Handman for weeks. Wynn Handman was the artistic director of the American Place Theatre, which produced the work of new playwrights, like Sam Shepard. Wynn Handman also taught acting classes, up one flight of stairs on Fifty-sixth Street off Seventh Avenue, right across town from me. Next door were a store that sold pianos and another that had motorcycles in the window. At the top of the stairs was one small room, with maybe fifty seats and a stage. Getting into Wynn Handman's acting classes was hard. Steve McQueen had gone there, so everyone wanted to study with Wynn Handman, who was in his middle age when I took his class.

Calling from the Plaza, I was able to arrange for an interview. Wynn Handman sat behind a desk with a light over it—he now pulled a chain to turn it off—in front of the stage. The stage lights were dim and he asked me to sit in a chair onstage. Then he asked me questions about why I wanted to take these classes of his, as if trying to figure out what kind of mind I had. I thought when I left that I'd seemed too confused and unsure, but a week later he called to tell me I'd got in. Now I was going to have a whole new existence.

The first class was on a Monday night, on October 3, 1966. I sat in the back row of seats and was so nervous I thought I would pass out. But I wasn't asked to do anything onstage that night. Almost everyone in the room, man or woman, was either pretty good-looking or else a real beauty. There was a blonde from Sweden who was clearly as maternal as she was seductive and opaque. She might well have gone straight into an Ingmar Bergman film that very night.

Wynn Handman himself had somewhat thinning light-brown hair and green eyes, and was tall. He was from Brooklyn; by the end of the first year he was calling me Alison Lettuce from Salinas. Like a benevolent father or a priest, he used the word "humanity" all the time, and he taught us how to talk to another person "moment to moment," which meant without being false or not present. Listening was the main point. I learned to listen from Wynn Handman. He made it his whole life to understand every sub-subtext inside every subtext of what a human being said and how he said it and also what he did and how. In his class he caught every single false gesture or thought or action or failure to listen. The first time I got up onstage, he asked me to do an improvisation with an actor so tall he was like a forest ranger. I talked incessantly, so that it was rather like a duel. There wasn't a way for this actor to out-wit me or to be more truthful than I was being, and after that night I was no longer so shy about going up there.

Nearly all the young men and women in class wanted to do scenes with me. One of them, a man named Christian, was a blond with a craggy face whom I worshipped because he played Holden Caulfield and James Agee just the way I'd imagined them to be from reading. When he read from Agee's *Letters to Father Flye* and looked up from his book at us and pronounced, "God bless you, Father Flye, and help me," we all wanted to help him.

When Christian wasn't onstage, he made up his own monologues, just in conversation. He talked and talked, and he talked some more, too much, as if life itself didn't exist unless he put everything he saw or had lived through or thought about or read into words and said them out loud. His good looks were imposing, in a blue-eyed, yellow-haired, worn-faced movie-hero way, so that one did listen. Still, he was tricky.

He talked fast, seductively, in a slightly Midwestern tone, sitting in a restaurant. But, unlike other talkers, while talking mostly to himself he seemed to see inside you at the same time—and he did it fast, intrusively. He could draw my attention to parts of myself I had made Herculean efforts to hide from him. Sitting across from him, to my own ear I might sound nearly buoyant, as opposed to downhearted; he'd interrupt and say, with such good humor that I'd think he was about to say something flattering, "My darling, you're the saddest girl in the whole world, the most woeful girl walking the streets of New York City."

People tended to defer to Christian, almost bow down, as if to royalty. Once, when Dill had gone to see Fellini's *Satyricon,* he had sat by chance in the row behind Christian and heard him ask the usher to go outside and get him a sandwich. What's more, Dill said disgustedly, the usher obeyed. Christian ate the sandwich right in the theatre: "salami, with Thousand Island dressing dripping off the paper and onto the floor."

One late afternoon, over a hamburger and hash browns, Christian said to me, his voice temporarily slowed down, volume lowered, and leaning over the red-and-white checkered tablecloth, "If we had a baby, it would be so sad it would just sit there and stare at the carpet." Then he laughed a long, harsh laugh, drank some more draft Michelob from a goblet, dazzled himself with his own words, and, mid-dazzle, fell into a dizzying state of romantic collapse, his fierce blue eyes looking around abusively at other people in the restaurant, and at me, too.

The tallest boyfriend I brought home to Dill was also from the acting class. He was a fellow named Clark. He was very tall—six feet six or more—and though his body looked like a cowhand's, his face didn't. His face was somewhat flat, not tough or outdoorsy, with small brown eyes, a little nose childishly tilted, and a small mouth, all of which gave a sweetness to his bigness and height. He often wore a pale suede jacket with fringe on it and, every single day, bluejeans with a big leather cowboy belt and cowboy boots with pointed toes and big heels—even in summer. He walked semi-slowly, but took small steps, had wide thighs, and was shy. He was from Montana.

Clark lived on Eighth Avenue, in the Fifties, in an apartment house that had a sign above it lit up with brassy lime-green neon lights. His bedroom in that apartment was big and barren, so that when I went in there all I saw was the large bed and Clark's tall body and his small face. He wasn't thin and he wasn't burly. He wasn't rowdy. He didn't talk much, never looked as if he belonged in New York City. He had a jittery naïveté that sometimes got him into trouble—and that's why, especially in Times Square, he seemed like a hapless country boy, just out of place. He listened carefully to everything I said—I would tell him how I felt I was not exactly in control of my mind—and he never gave an easy, glib answer. His voice was rather high. If he'd had a loud, deep voice, he would have been scary. Clark's tallness, his cowboy trappings, the big thighs he had, and the way he was from some little town in a part of the country I didn't understand, where maybe they sang "Red River Valley" over a campfire, maybe to a harmonica straight out of *The Grapes of Wrath*—all that made me want to be with him in his head, wherever it was.

Clark's mother had hanged herself when he was a boy. The only story he told me about home was of the time he walked into the cellar where she had done this and saw her hanging from a rope. He went to that therapy—popular at the time—where all the patients got together and screamed. It was unnerving to think of Clark screaming in some therapy room in New York City.

What we did was rehearse scenes for acting class in Dill's and my apartment, sitting on two director's chairs facing the front door, during the day, when Dill was at work. Everyone in class—there were thirty of us—looked forward, they told us, to watching Clark and me together on the little stage. We did a scene from William Saroyan's "Hello Out There," where the young man was in prison and the girl brought him food. In the scene, Clark was exactly like that character—all by himself, despite the girl. We'd spent about twenty hours rehearsing it the week before. The girl had to be entirely with him but somehow all alone, too.

On Saturday nights, Clark would come over to pick me up— he was gentlemanly that way, and Dill approved of him—and take me back to his room on Eighth Avenue. There was a little bedside table with a pipe and a tinfoil package of hashish on it, which Clark smoked; I smoked it, too, but only with him. I'd never smoked anything like that before—only Kents—and never did it again. Once I do a particular thing with one person, I can't do it again with anyone else. In the tenth grade, at the Annie Wright Seminary, Miss Capelle taught me Latin. She was twenty-two, with a German accent from Germany, and tall, with a fawnlike legginess, her long back to the class, writing with white chalk on the blackboard. To this day, I hate it when anyone else uses Latin quotations, because Latin words are *hers*. I could never order half a roast spring chicken with anyone except Dill. Clark's hand looked small when he held the pipe in front of his wide, hairlessly smooth chest then brought it up to his mouth to smoke.

Hedy Lamarr's son Tony was another of my fellow acting students. He gave me a set of his mother's towels, faded gray, with "HL" in magenta script. For years those towels hung over every shower curtain I had, first in New York and then in Los Angeles. In my bedroom in Palo Alto, I had watched Hedy Lamarr on my little black-and-white television set: that dark, dark hair and the light eyes and the pretty, small nose. Tony had it, too, but without the prettiness, or the foreign accent. Hedy Lamarr was born in Austria, where Lanz nightgowns—the flannel ones with the hearts—came from, and Tony told me his grandmother, his mother's mother, had started the Lanz nightgown company in Vienna.

Tony was big, and called me Baby Susie, after an unattended-to rag doll I kept facedown on a chair on Fifty-seventh Street. Tony was so good to me that the next spring I left Dill and the apartment for a week and went to live with Tony in a one-bedroom sublet apartment in Fort Lee, New Jersey. That week, we took the bus back and forth to class and one day painted the bathroom orange. Even after we moved back to New York, we wrote our own scenes together. I liked best the scenes I wrote for myself, one about a conversation with a psychiatrist about suicide, pronounced "cidey-Sue," with a Bob Dylan lyric—"It's all right, Ma, it's life and life only"—in the background. A tribute to drollery: everyone agreed.

Tony had a dog he called Tony, like a shadow self, and Tony and Tony were like brothers. Tony the dog was big and dark-haired, too, part Labrador, and they went nearly everywhere together (not to class), with Tony riding a bicycle and Tony running after him through New York City streets. They moved from apartment to sublet apartment, one of which had a round bed in it, where we stayed inside for days at a time listening to "Ruby Tuesday" over and over again. One Saturday in July, on the Upper West Side, Tony lost Tony (he may have been stolen), and this still makes me more heartsick than I get over many lost humans. Soon afterward, the human Tony moved back to the greater desolation of Los Angeles.

Toward the end of my household with Dill, a boy I called Stevie the Greek put all the dirty dinner dishes in the bathtub, blue-and-white plates with white suds around and over them, and then we watched all the little pieces of meat and other food sliding off and floating in the oily water. Stevie the Greek was nineteen and sort of a hoodlum, or pretended he was—and he was, sort of—and when I saw him for the first time, at the bus stop on Fifty-seventh and Third Avenue, and he saw me, there wasn't a way we weren't going to get in bed together. Although we had tea—literally tea, at Horn & Hardart's—for weeks before he barged into my apartment, when Dill was at work, and we finally did. Even though I was with him, opening the door for him with my key, he seemed to be barging in anyway, and he said, "This is it, Rose." He said it like a bad guy. No one had ever called me that before.

His given name was Stavros. Once, he took me to eat his mother's Greek cooking in Astoria, Queens; and on Fifty-seventh Street one afternoon he said, "Listen to this, Rose!," and I heard Richie Havens for the first time: "Got those sit down can't cry Oh Lord I want to die blues."

. . .

The summer before Dill moved out, I walked across town to Bendel's and bought eight nightgowns made in Italy, each of them different and all of them long. The saleswoman thought I was getting married, but all I was doing was buying my summer wardrobe. Nightgowns were so much nicer than the cheap little minidresses everyone was wearing. They felt more private. I was planning on not leaving the house. Dill was thirteen years older than I was, and older than anyone else I hung around with in those days, so he was the adult. Sometimes when I actually called him Mother to his face, he might say, "Alison, I'm not your mother"—but in a practical, matter-of-fact way, never with impatience. What he really was, maybe, was a wife, or a mother-husband hybrid at least. He was the only truly husbandlike man I've known, all in all.

Indoors, with Dill, I could wear my nightgowns night and day and not worry about what strangers would think. Dill would come home from work, bringing porterhouse steaks, and tell me about the airlessness and stench of the subway. We decided that we didn't have to take a car or an airplane to a real beach. We took cool baths instead, one at a time, with the other sitting on the bathroom sink, smoking, legs dangling. By the time it was my turn, Dill might open the window for a moment, for the breeze, and he'd move the soap dish a bit, to make room for a gin-and-tonic, with a slice of lime. After my bath, I'd change into my dinner nightgown, often a black silky one, and, when he'd cooked the steaks in the broiler behind shuttered, smoky kitchen doors, we'd eat them at a round wooden table in a corner of our room, with the central air-conditioning turned up. It was more privacy than we would have had at Lake Tahoe, with waiters and other intruders.

Because Dill was my mother and not my lover, when we lived together and I had those boyfriends I would spend the night at their apartments and then go home to Dill. There was real, undamageable pleasure in going home to Dill: the routine dinners, our exclusivity, and the assurance that he—my ideal mother—was not going to turn on me, no matter what I did or failed to do. At night our twin beds were along one wall lengthwise, my head to his head, and we'd turn the lights off and play games, like guessing the name of our elderly neighbor, whose first initial, E., was on her front door. We would think of all the "E" names we could: Edith, Evelyn, Elaine, then Evangeline, finally Enid, and roll around in our separate beds, convulsed with laughter. I missed all that after he left.

When Dill moved out, the next July, in 1968—he insisted on his own life—I slammed the door on summer. I had all those nightgowns professionally laundered, wrapped them in tissue paper, and put them in a suitcase under the bed. I didn't want anything around that even looked like a sundress. Then I walked over to the Woolworth's on Third Avenue (I ate the last orange Creamsicle from the freezer on the way, as a goodbye to summer) and bought enough skeins of pale-pink and pale-blue yarn to knit a blanket big enough to cover a double bed. I dragged the yarn, in two large plastic bags, through the sticky air back to my apartment, turned the air-conditioning up as high as it would go, and put on a long-sleeved gray cable-knit cardigan over a short, pleated flannel skirt and black tights. I put Shalimar, not Jean Naté, on the insides of my wrists, because the smell reminded me of ice-skating rinks. Then, with the fake chill all around me, I sat in a director's chair right next to the air-conditioner and knitted. I liked the feeling of the woolly, cake-colored yarn between my fingers, and the cold air coming up from the machine. I liked knowing how to knit the squares together with my masterly blanket stitch.

Every once in a while, I would put the knitting needles aside and smoke a Kent. When I absolutely had to, I took off my winter clothes, threw on something lightweight but non-revealing, and walked a block and a half over to D'Agostino's for some food. I did this fast, because daylight, heat, bare legs, halter tops, and flesh-at-large were like a rebuke.

Some mornings, I took a longer break and went to the Mayflower, across from Schrafft's, for Cream of Wheat, poached eggs on buttered whole-wheat toast, and hot chocolate with whipped cream—an homage to winter. One day, Philip Roth— dark, wavy hair, tallish—was there by himself. *Portnoy's Complaint* had come out not long before, and he looked solitary, in an enviable way, as if his own thinking were more than sufficient company. He was a reminder that each of us had certifiable permission to do *anything*. If Portnoy had "fucked [his] own family's dinner," I could deform summer into winter if I felt like it. I came back home to the pink and blue knitted squares, which I'd left spread out on the bed, to measure how much I had accomplished; got dressed for the cold again, and sat down to knit some more. The cat knew what to do, too; he sat in his winter position: under a Chinese lamp, where he could feel the heat from the light bulb.

. . .

I went to see Dr. Cederquist in his townhouse in the East Nineties. Back when I was eighteen, he was a man in his early fifties, a psychiatrist. I had seen a few psychiatrists, but pretty much loathed all of them. I had put a camellia flower in my hair that day, and when I sat down in the armchair he said, "What a pretty flower you have in your hair," as if talking to a little girl. He said it in this odd voice that was somewhat Middle American (he was from Jamestown, New York); his voice was odd also because he'd had damage to his ear, from being in the Navy in the Second World War, and wore a hearing aid. When he said the flower was pretty, I knew right away I would know him always, which I did until he died, in 1999.

Periodically during these New York years—Duncan, Baby Bob, Dill, acting—I would go up there to see Dr. Cederquist with brown paper bags filled with the food I had been eating, to show him the actual Hydrox cookies and the Sara Lee orange cakes and Sara Lee pecan coffee cakes so that he could see, literally see, what was on my mind a great deal of the time. Cederquist would look at the food and smile and approve of it in his gentle manner, as he had the flower, and in at least a small way I had a kinder attitude to the flower, to the food.

One winter night in Saint-Moritz, after I'd walked all around a lake with a tall German—I never did get his name straight, but I had to have him or die—I had gone on to spend the morning with him in a hotel room with white ruffled curtains, and I came back to New York pregnant. My mother said over the telephone from California that if I attempted to have the baby alone I could go on welfare. Dr. Cederquist, as if to remind me of all the things I wouldn't be able to give the baby, said, "But what about her ice-skating lessons?" I didn't have her, but from time to time I thought about that pronoun.

Sometimes on the way to an appointment with Dr. Cederquist I would buy a stack of Dunkin' Donuts in the Fifty-ninth Street and Lexington subway station—I liked the glazed ones—and after a conversation with Baby Bob about not eating them after all, I'd leave them in the bag in the phone booth, and then, after the session with Dr. Cederquist, go back and retrieve them. I liked Dr. Cederquist so much I wanted, for the first time, to be known—at least somewhat—by that old a person.

Dill took a black-and-white photograph of me in front of Cederquist's townhouse, full-length, wearing a double-breasted dark-brown fall coat with a wool paisley scarf tied around my head. The print Dill made was eleven by fourteen, big, and I gave it to Cederquist for Christmas. He said he'd keep it in a safe place. Cederquist had another townhouse, later—this one on East Seventy-first, between Park and Lexington. One fall, that house was empty, there were just workmen in it, and Baby Bob and I, out for a walk and passing by, went *into the house.*

The kitchen was on the first floor. We told the workmen that we were Dr. Cederquist's children; they believed us. We found a can of Campbell's tomato soup on a shelf and opened it, and found a pan and lit the stove and cooked it. Then we got scared, and left without eating it. In one room, we saw a very large portrait of a young man whom we imagined to be the real child of Dr. Cederquist. He appeared calm.

I sent Baby Bob to Dr. Cederquist and he, too, went there for a long time. For a while, Baby Bob had great affection for Dr. Cederquist. Now, however, three decades after stopping, he has a different view. "He was just this old man who couldn't hear and sat in a chair," he says. "His hearing aid was making that noise—we were convinced he'd turned it off and he read lips. He was a wealth of information. He knew *all* about the Battle of Agincourt and Henry V. That was useful information. We'd get useful information for an hour—it was like watching PBS—and then we'd go on as if nothing happened. Look, Alison, you were sleeping in the Park, for God's sake, and pulling on your eyelashes. You were obviously out of your mind, and Duncan was really out of his mind, and probably dangerous, and where was Dr. Cederquist? *I mean, you were sleeping in the Park with Duncan. What was he doing? What kind of therapy was that?*"

I went on seeing Dr. Cederquist nevertheless. Even when I moved to Los Angeles, I talked to him on the telephone and wrote him letters. When I returned to New York, in 1977, I went to see him right away. He had saved one of my letters; I could see my large handwriting on the envelope every week when he opened his big black binder. I went to see him for another twenty-two years.

I haven't slept in a park since 1964.

WAITING FOR SOMETHING TO HAPPEN

West Hollywood in the seventies was mostly flat and mostly ugly, with mostly short buildings, a cheesy little town within a city, not that many palm trees. I saw it in a flatter, slower-paced, closer-to-the-pavement way than other people did, though, because I was walking a lot; I didn't drive. The sun seemed hotter to me there, because of the walking. The only reason I'd gone to Los Angeles was that I had had an interview in New York with a French movie director. He'd liked my face and in auditions he'd liked my acting. So did the producers. A round-trip airplane ticket, a room at the Beverly Wilshire, and a screen test were arranged. All this seemed like a good idea. I thought I would at last have proof of my existence if I were in this French director's movie. Or initial proof.

The Beverly Wilshire is right in the middle of the shopping part of Beverly Hills. It isn't pretty the way the Beverly Hills Hotel is, with those pink bungalows, but I'd wanted to stay at the Wilshire—I had a choice—so that I could walk to a drugstore for emergency mascara, or get some food in a market, as if

I were in New York City. It's weird to take taxis in Los Angeles, although I took them the whole time I lived there, about seven years. They sort of got to know me at the Beverly Hills Cab Company, and I liked that odd Western diction some of those Los Angeles taximen had. They knew their way around the whole landscape, were proud to tell you all about it, what grew where. They had permanent suntans, especially on their left arms, and hair no darker than light brown. They were a brand of human being I'd never met before, and there are still a few left.

The French director's movie was canceled and so was my screen test. All the decision-makers had a fight about money and went back to Europe. In a way, I didn't care. The disintegration of possibility was a reprieve, even a relief, because when something I wanted badly actually happened I didn't seem to know how to do anything except wreck it, and this time I didn't have to do the wrecking myself. George Trow later said, and I have this written down in dark-red ink in the drawer of the table next to my bed, "If you were successful you wouldn't know who you were."

I left the Beverly Wilshire then and went to stay with my Latin teacher from the Annie Wright Seminary, who now lived up on Coldwater Canyon, in Beverly Hills. I hadn't seen Miss Capelle for twelve years, though I thought of her *(Odi et amo)* often, and now she had a husband and school-age children. No one was home during the day, so I listened to the radio in the kitchen, or read, or walked up and down Coldwater—past normal-looking ranch houses that families would live in, with front lawns. Meanwhile, from New York, Wynn Handman was setting up meetings for me with movie directors he'd known in the fifties. I took taxis out to the studios to see them. All of them knew that I was well trained and serious, because Wynn Handman had told them so.

One director had sandy-colored hair that wouldn't stay close to his head. The hair was as energetic as he was; what he hated most was stasis. Despite the willful joie de vivre, he spoke slowly, in a hushed, just-for-you, irresistible voice. He had a way of making you think you were inside his mind and he was inside yours—a grandiose, actory, contagious intensity. When I didn't have any money for a taxi, I walked all the way along Santa Monica Boulevard out to Samuel Goldwyn Studios just to hear that voice talk to me. The walk took about an hour. This man was good at making you feel like a vigorous part of his vigorous life, even in half an hour and from across a desk. He transformed and gently bullied everyone around him by *understanding,* or making you think he understood, every nuance of what you said and didn't say. To myself, I referred to him as the Man Who Understands.

One thing he understood completely was my amusement when he gave me a ticket to the Academy Awards, and got one of his closest director friends to accompany me. To celebrate the Man Who Understands's nomination for best director, I bought a slinky but not too slithery black dress from Holly's Harp, a new dress shop on Sunset. Still, there was this little unidentifiable persistent something that the Man Who Understands didn't understand at that point about the humans, and maybe that's why he didn't win the award that year. Nonetheless I gave him a trophy: a silver cup with "Life Force" engraved on it.

One time, three of these movie directors—they'd all grown up and worked in New York—were in one office at one studio, jacaranda trees with purple flowers outside the windows, and they all laughed together and seemed to be liking life. The funniest one, a stocky redhead with a flat face and a wide nose, handed the other two a little machine that laughed when you tilted or shook it. I sat in a leather armchair by myself while the redhead, the Man Who Understands, and a shy director with short, tightly curled black hair sat on a soft sofa, and we all laughed harder whenever the laughing machine laughed.

.   .   .

I met Billy the Fish in a large brown house on Beverly Drive while I was staying with Miss Capelle on Coldwater. A friend invited me up to this brown house, where friends of hers lived—we arrived and sat around the kitchen listlessly, as if we were all waiting for something.

Billy the Fish was wearing a powder-blue windbreaker when he walked in the back door, carrying bags of groceries. Because of that too pale jacket, too Southern California, and the straight, long blond hair flopping around his head, and because of a certain air of separateness, at first I thought he was the delivery boy from a grocery store. I had one of those instantaneous, fixated, have-to-be-closer-to-that-blond-hair-or-else-give-up-and-die feelings; irrational. He *looked* like he got The Point, without my or anyone's having to say what The Point was. I felt sorry that he would leave quickly after the delivery. But then that relief: he knew everyone, he wasn't a delivery boy.

Billy was twenty-two but seemed like an older man, a grown man, with a heaviness of spirit. After dinner, he and I went over to his house, in West Hollywood, and I stayed with him, pretty much, for seven years. It was on Hilldale Avenue, a seedy, old, gray, flat-roofed house half a block south of the Sunset Strip. It

was a shack, a slum, a crummy little falling-down house—
purposely run-down, it seemed. It had clearly been tormented
into looking like that. Inside, the house was dark, with low
ceilings, and with decaying, rickety old furniture. It seemed
safer not to sit down. A couch against the wall was covered in a
scratchy brown-and-black weave with a gold synthetic thread
in it. It would be hard to imagine an uglier couch. Across from
it was another couch. This one had been, at one time, a cheap
white leather sofa, and it still was, except that now some of it
was all ripped up, with stuffing coming out. It was truly a
thing rotting. There was carpet, a dark color. It was hard to tell
if it was green or brown and it was so worn that later on, no
matter how much I vacuumed it, and I did that a lot, it never
got brighter. In one corner were a brown table and a few brown
chairs that no one ever would have touched. This dinette set
looked as if it had been left outside for years: it sat all by itself
in the corner, as if no one ever left a coat or a handbag on it.
Billy called the house Camp Suicide.

Billy the Fish and I had a sort of domestic life in this seedy
house on Hilldale. The only *real* boyfriend I ever had (a live-in-
a-house-together lover) I had there. I cleaned and cleaned, especially the kitchen floor, with a brown wooden brush with hard
bristles. I did this in a discarded short yellow slip of Francine's;
a ritual garment. Billy wrote me a note: "Alo is a maid and only
a maid." I was so nervous in Los Angeles that I couldn't learn to
drive, so Billy took the laundry—scary old green towels, with
my HL towels—to the Fluff & Fold on Santa Monica, and I
walked to the Sun Bee, seven minutes away on Sunset, for groceries. Night or day, I was the only one walking: blazing sun,
New York shoes, long striped knit dress, too thin. One day
Bruce Dern, whom I'd met at the Actors Studio, yelled at me
from his car, "Smile, you fuckin' asshole! *Smile!*"

The kitchen was big, a real room, windows over the sink, an old refrigerator with a handle like a car door's, a Formica table and four or five wooden chairs. I tossed Spic 'n' Span or one of those cleansers on the floor and put water from a large jar on top of that. People were always coming in and out of the Hilldale house—no locked doors. Ernie Kovacs's daughter Betty, who came over nearly every day in her black Buick, was a witness to my cleaning. "You were waiting for something to happen that never did," she said to me later. "In the meantime, you were cleaning." Billy had been married to Betty's younger sister when they were both in their teens, and their child was around Hilldale sometimes, a little girl who lived with Betty's grandmother, the mother of Ernie Kovacs; Ernie Kovacs was dead by then. I cleaned the ashtrays all the time, too. "Like a waitress," Betty said.

I wanted Billy to want to marry me. He not only had the silkiest pale-blond hair but was darkly funny. He had one leg that was slightly lame from polio, and he limped fairly badly, which was endearing, because the rest of his body was more or less like Burt Lancaster's; Burt Lancaster was his father. Billy himself—his own presence—drew all kinds of people to come by to visit him at Hilldale, just to drink with him and try to figure out if they were in his good graces or not. "I mean, let's face it," one of them told me much, much later, "in that house Bill was the main attraction. He was the *main* attraction. And weren't you some kind of damsel in distress there? You made coffee, if I remember. Didn't you make coffee? You tried to be like a servant, isn't that right? You tried—I mean, you tried to make things work." I did and still they didn't.

The chances of my losing my footing with Billy never diminished, and sometimes I took five or six blue Valiums during the day, along with an Eskatrol, which was a kind of speed that Daddy had prescribed for me. Billy drank too much, and sometimes blacked out, or he made pots of coffee. There was something innately glamorous and sad about his presence. He dominated everyone around him. Billy's father had always called him Billy the Bum, but I called him Billy the Fish. He floated slimly through a dim aquarium place, the other fish-friends flickering about him. I called him Billy the Fish because it was as if he lived in his own element, as if the air that other people breathed were different from whatever he breathed. He was like a blond modified fish in a bowl who came up for other people's air, curious, but not very often. He'd talk to you when he came up, but he couldn't stay up for long or he'd die. That's why he is now dead. He died in 1998, at the age of forty-nine. In 1970, at twenty-two, he was bored by what most of the people said to him. He'd interrupt them and say, "Look at Alo. Isn't Alo pretty?"

We weren't alone at Hilldale. Billy had known most of the little gang around the house since high school—Billy worshippers. A sassy redhead, a painter, had a hard crush on Billy. She called him Bill. She painted in the studio out back, where laundresses once professionally ironed sheets for the Doheny Estate. Too early in the morning, we could hear her heavy shoes on the kitchen floor.

Billy's best friend hid pastel-colored blackout pills (we called them B O P S for short) under the cushions of the ugly brown couch, so we had to hunt for them, like Easter eggs: Nembutal, Tuinol, Placidyl (the green ones). "My mind was locked up and docked with his," he says of Billy now. In the mornings, I took the speed Daddy sent me in the mail: envelopes of capsules, some multicolored spillage in a corner, which you could pour into your mouth like jello mix.

"Was there any hope for me then?" I ask the best friend now.

"Not really," he says. "Except for the fact that you kept those notebooks."

There was a large, middle-aged man who, though he had a ranch in Arizona as big as New Hampshire, lived in the tiny apartment above the garage. He would drop in for a drink and a look around, then go out and back upstairs, where he drank Martinis double-fisted and guarded his collection of country-and-western albums: Loretta Lynn before she was Loretta Lynn.

Billy would say to me, now and again, "Now, *Alo*. What are you *doing* knowing *any* of us."

Billy the Fish had what I called " 'It's a lie' syndrome." It was a joke to him to take something away. He used to say, "It's a li-ie," kind of the way Jack Nicholson in *The Shining* later said, "Here's Johnny," but without the visible axe. After a straight-forward statement about domestic matters—"Alo, we're going to the beach house for dinner"—he'd go into the melody: "It's a li-ie." Though we might wind up going to the beach house for dinner after all. Or not. Ambiguity was a large part of Billy the Fish; in his mind, things he said were true and untrue at the same time. He wanted other people to know it: as a warning, an attack on their illusions; or to let them know he knew that they themselves were mostly lying all the time anyway. He knew how to flatten a person's airs of falsity. It was his way of winning the human lying contest.

Billy had a blue Volkswagen—a convertible—and would drive me around with him on his errands; sometimes he took me to the movies: Truffaut, Bertolucci, *Five Easy Pieces,* Louis Malle's *The Fire Within*. My heart liked him. I thought of Billy and Los Angeles as one entity. I still do.

On Billy's twenty-third birthday, one of the Hilldale guys gave him a burgundy cashmere scarf. When he opened the package, his hair and his white shirt all messy in his mother's house, in a room with pale-pink quilting over all the walls and ceiling, like a padded cell, Billy said to me, about receiving the scarf, "T's to my E's," meaning "tears to my eyes." When you were around him all the time, you could understand his abbreviations without thinking about them. I think he abbreviated his words because he had such a disdain for life that he wanted to describe it in the shortest way possible. On that birthday night, he also told me, as we were running up a stairway at his father's house, "Alo, if only I were ready we could have the greatest love affair of all time." All I could see was his back, so I didn't know what to say. I didn't say anything.

Billy didn't pay much attention to who was hanging out at Hilldale, just walked around in his underpants and dried his floppy blond hair by the blasting heater in the living room. Ninety degrees in summer didn't make any difference. He would stand there in his underpants and dry that hair. Girls who bleached their hair, brown-haired girls who wanted to become blond, would lose composure when they looked at that blond hair, and I got to be with it all night, a lightness in the dark at any hour. In the bedroom, Billy's hair was mine, in the sense that I could rearrange it and be with it any time of day, since Billy didn't get up until noon on the average. I would be up and dressed, but go back and lie beside him in my clothes while he was blacked out.

Late at night he would try to write, or he watched sports on the junky TV on the edge of the ugly brown couch. Not too much later, he would finish a screenplay—sports in it, *The Bad*

News Bears—that when it became a movie got him a lot of praise. Meanwhile, though the bedroom wasn't that small, the bed seemed to take up most of the space. It was a king-size bed, a whole room within a room, permeated by the smell of un-smoked, unfiltered Camels rocking in a glass ashtray, spilling on the sheet, little bits of tobacco in my mouth from his mouth. I smoked my Kents, but the Camels and sex in that big bed with Billy and his blond hair were an off-kilter dream-come-true, and it was mine.

I never got bored with Billy. I waited all day for it to be night, to be in bed with him. The complete truth is: the most *normale* I ever was—approaching the phenomenon I called "normal pie," this thing men and women get married about—was with him, because I wanted to be with him. It wasn't sexu-ally sexy sex, or a thing apart from him.

Sometimes Francine would come over to Hilldale in the after-noons and we'd all take a nap. Francine was living in Holly-wood, in the late sixties and early seventies, in a Spanish-style building on Orange Grove. It was the kind of apartment we all came over to. Some of the many men milling around her there were dependent on her kindness. Even though Francine weighed about ninety pounds then and wore cut-on-the-bias dresses and was ten years younger than those men were, they thought of her as some kind of mother, and she was. Edward G. Robinson Jr. lived next door. "He always wore his blue terry-cloth bathrobe when he came by," Francine said. "He had on black socks usually. I don't think I ever saw him dressed. He would sit on my long blue-flowered sofa in that robe with his arms spread on the back of the sofa as if he were holding court. He looked just like his father, but he was taller. He'd recite lines from his father's movies verbatim. People said he always carried a gun. Everyone was afraid of him. He would have shot anyone else, but he loved me." John Drew Barrymore was there all the time, too. "We had tea in my teacups," Francine said. "They were blue and gold with little orange fish on them. He knew all about teacups. Every time he walked in he looked as if he'd been living in the desert for the past ten years." Of course, Francine did not sleep with these men, not after all her mother's impeccable tutelage, and, anyway, they were content just to be in her aura. She cooked for them, too. She made bacon-and-spinach salads, especially for Eddie Jr. The man she really liked, though, was an actor who lived downstairs. He gave her his brown suede jacket, and when she got married she had me keep it and I had it in my closet for years.

When Elvis Presley performed at the Fox Theatre in Atlanta, in 1956, Francine hadn't gone to see him. She hated his dyed black hair and thought he looked "redneck country tacky"—like a hood. "Mother would never have let me go out with a boy like that," she said. But in Hollywood, in 1968, Francine and a ballerina friend were having dinner in a restaurant when one of Elvis's bodyguards invited the friend—he thought she looked like Priscilla Presley—to go visit Elvis in Palm Springs. The friend was scared, so Francine went along as a chaperon, even though she still thought he was a hood.

The weekend included a tour of Elvis's closet, which, Francine said, "was like a holy place, about fifteen feet long, with all his white jackets—twenty-five or thirty of them—perfectly spaced on perfect hangers. He was so proud of it." The one time Elvis, the friend, and Francine went out of the house, along with five bodyguards, was to buy Francine's friend a dress at I. Magnin. They drove in three Cadillacs, "like a funeral procession." Francine was fixing her hair in the back seat of the middle Cadillac, which Elvis was driving, and, she says, "I parted my hair, made a wave on the right side, and put on lip gloss—I was watching him watching me."

Back at the house, Elvis and the girls got dressed up. Elvis put on one of his white jackets from the closet, and white trousers. Then they all sat on the sofa with the bodyguards until one of the bodyguards got up and put on a few of Elvis's records. The friend danced with Elvis. Francine didn't really want to dance with Elvis, but he talked her into it by saying, "You have to. One day you can tell your grandchildren that you danced with me to 'Blue Suede Shoes.'" They jitterbugged to "Blue Suede Shoes" two or three times.

When Francine and her friend were packing to leave, the head bodyguard asked Francine for her telephone number. Elvis called her a few times, but she never did see him. "There just wasn't anything that appealed to me about him whatsoever," she said. "And he was so sad." Francine never thinks anything she's ever done was a mistake.

When Francine and Billy and I took a nap together on Hilldale, we would all three pretend to be asleep in the dark bedroom. Then we'd smoke our Camels and Kents surrounded by cellophane wrappings on the sheets. On those afternoons, I felt complete, bookended on both sides by two different kinds of blond hair, two kinds of protection—an unending pleasure that would never wear out.

In the living room on Hilldale there was a small fake Christmas tree with fake oranges on it, which Burt Lancaster had given to us one Christmas as a nice gesture, but that tree was one concrete thing that said to me, "Life does not make sense." Sometimes Billy and I went up to the house Billy had grown up in, in Bel-Air—a faux river ran through it, a "water feature"—and his father's black maids took care of us and cooked.

Sometimes two of Billy's three sisters were there, and we'd *do* things with them—get out of Hilldale. I'd feel safe. I wanted to marry all of it. Billy's father often recommended my coming out of depression: just doing it, no fooling around. When he told me not to be crazy, in his big kitchen, in that lilting, authoritative Burt Lancaster cadence—all the words going up, and then all the words going down—I almost wasn't crazy after all. I guess I wanted to marry *him*.

There were other houses. Billy's mother's house, above Sunset Plaza, was a modern one, plain on the outside. Billy's mother was of Swedish origin and she had a small nose, just like Billy's, and blond hair. Her name was Norma, but behind her back, to me, Billy called her Normal. Billy's mother was nice to me. She wasn't ever not nice. The only normal California-girl thing I did in the time I lived in L.A. was sit by the pool with Billy's mother. We didn't really have a conversation, but she might say, "Billy's handsomer than Burt!" He wasn't, but I didn't disagree.

One day, Norma gave me a forties-like, one-piece white bathing suit to wear, since I had never put on a bathing suit by the pool, and I looked good in it, as if someone had made it for me. So that day I felt like a real live L.A. girl. That might have been better than living your whole life as a real girl and then not remembering it too well, having it not mean much to you. That day, one of Billy's sisters joined me and Norma by the pool. Joanna was lying on the diving board, talking across the water to where we sat, approving of the white bathing suit with vehemence, and added that my face looked like Gregory Peck's in the Hitchcock movie where he can't remember anything. She meant this as a high compliment.

It was on his Smith Corona typewriter that Billy wrote "Alo is a maid and only a maid" in the center of a sheet of typing paper, adding, "but she is also a great Coke and lemon maker. And she is also a skinny, a minny, a pretty." Lower on the same page I typed: "This was written by Bill Lancaster at his Hilldale house, which was just cleaned by Alison Rose, the maid." I began writing notes to Billy on the dailyness at Hilldale.

I was in the shower one Easter morning, mildew on the shower curtain, when Billy the Fish said in a loud voice, "Want to go and see B.L., Alo? Want to be *nor-mal?*" We drove out to the Malibu beach house. Tuesday Weld was swimming in the swimming pool, which was right in front of the beach. Billy's father was sitting in a chair watching her. He had this *big* smile on his face, and his white Burt Lancaster teeth were glistening in the sun. Things felt somewhat sane on holidays there. The dinners were at a dinner table, and there were the sisters, an attempt at family, with a real leader, a crowned head of Europe, in Southern California. Before he was a movie star, Burt Lancaster was a flying-trapeze artist in the circus.

Anybody who knew us at the time would agree that what Billy said all the time was "What if, Alo, what *if,*" in a teasing tone. Then he'd laugh hard, to himself. He'd say "What *if*" to me, or to anyone, and not finish, just leave the person in midair. Often Billy would say the word "cringe," with a wince, and would cross himself. He was brought up loosely as a Catholic. All of us loved him, in one way or another, but he couldn't feel it, I don't think.

George Trow, who once, fourteen years ago, sent me four eight-by-ten glossies, publicity stills for old Burt Lancaster movies, at another time said to me, in his giving-orders voice, "*Darling,* I don't *have* any feelings." And that, for me, gave not-having-any-feelings a permanent imprint. One photograph was, unavoidably, a still from *From Here to Eternity;* another was of B.L. with Montgomery Clift. I'd told George a lot about life on Hilldale. He liked crowned heads of Europe himself. Those photographs were a good present. (Despite his not having any *feelings,* he thought about who'd been important to me.) If Billy couldn't feel that we loved him, he looked, however, as if he did in fact have feelings. His entire face and his little blue cross-examining eyes sometimes looked as if he loved me. Definitely.

The last time I saw Billy was about ten years ago, on a working visit to L.A., around one-thirty in the morning. We hadn't seen each other for thirteen years. He was sitting at the bar in the Regent Beverly Wilshire, his hair still light in the semi-darkness, and he said in an infuriated outburst, "*My* father was Burt Lancaster! He was *crazy!* He was blazing all over the *world!*" He said it as if there was no way to recover from such a blow, from such an impairment, as if he meant to make clear why he couldn't love me the way I had wanted him to. After he left, I sat all alone and wrote down what he'd said on a little hotel pad of paper the bartender gave me.

*   *   *

The Actors Studio was an unnoticeable house on a small hill in West Hollywood, a half-hour walk from Hilldale, and off Sweetzer Avenue, a steep drop-down onto De Longpre. It was a white frame house and had a grape arbor on one side. William

S. Hart, the cowboy star, lived there when West Hollywood was orchards. In the sixties, the Actors Studio was made from what had been his garage, in the back, and it had a real stage and regular theatre seats, about seventy of them. The people who showed up there to teach in the early seventies knew every infinitesimal thing about serious acting. There was Actor's Night on Mondays, Playwright's Unit on Tuesday nights, and Director's Unit on Wednesday nights. I attended all three nights. This was my job when I was not a maid.

Lee Strasberg pointed to me one Monday night and said, "Shut the front door," and some people got pretty excited—it was a big deal when Strasberg said anything to an actor. When Strasberg wasn't around, there would be various moderators on Actor's Night: Shelley Winters sometimes, buxom and giddy, near-crazily brilliant. I could listen to her talk about acting all night. Mark Rydell seemed as if he would take us all home to his house, maybe even to New York, where he came from, and take care of us. When he'd analyze someone's performance, he was like the voice of the New York Psychoanalytic Institute (in a nice way).

Sydney Pollack, who looked and sounded like a real live unnarcissistic, regular man, whether he was or not, was a moderator, too. His *They Shoot Horses, Don't They?* was the last movie I'd seen in New York; it had seemed to me that Pollack had an extensive comprehension of what was sordid and *triste*. He wrote me a note that began, "Your work at the studio has everybody talking." And Bruce Dern, a compulsive truth-teller as a moderator, said to me one night in the driveway, almost yelling, like a coach, or an off-balance sergeant in a movie, "You have a million-dollar *face.*" Like "Smile, you fuckin' asshole," it was his way of telling me he wouldn't permit me to look sad.

One Tuesday night, at the Playwright's Unit, this very tall, sullen-looking, unnaturally gorgeous, actively beautiful man was leaning against the door of the theatre as I came in. I recognized him right away from *Adventures in Paradise:* Gardner McKay. When I was sent to the Annie Wright Seminary, the school psychologist had had to get involved in the crush I had on him. Gardner McKay was my savior, I told him, the way Jesus Christ was the Savior of the other Annie Wright girls, and I would get better only if I could watch Gardner McKay on television the way they sang to Jesus in the chapel. The psychologist, a good-looking man himself, with short gray hair, didn't think my attachment to an actor on television was unreasonable, and allowed me to watch *Adventures in Paradise* once, and without the consent of the headmistress or the housemother. Somehow that was enough.

I stopped at the door where Gardner was leaning. He stayed right there, didn't move away. His face was more noble now, a little world-weary. His whole self seemed as heavyhearted and despondent as it had on TV. And my attachment thing slipped into a tie between us right there, by the Studio door. I had been absolutely right in my room in Palo Alto and at Annie Wright. He had that same displaced look he'd had on the boat in Tahiti, where parts of *Adventures in Paradise* were filmed. When he said his name, introducing himself, he had a slight stammer, an awkwardness. "Never be famous for the wrong thing," he said to me during our conversation, a warning. He meant his having been an actor, which he now wasn't anymore; he was a playwright and short-story writer. This was Playwright's Unit night, after all. He had written a play about a retarded teen-age boy and now asked me to play the boy. I played the boy. Over the next few weeks, we did research together, like driving out

to visit a hospital for retarded boys, who climbed all over Gardner because he was so tall, even up onto his shoulders, as if he
were a tree.

We performed *Tomby* at the Actors Studio and on television—retitled "Me"—for PBS, and Geraldine Fitzgerald, who
had played the girl Heathcliff rejected in *Wuthering Heights,*
played my mother in it. That was an odd, ironic, extra chal-
lenge in acting, and a memory that, years later, saved me in
New York, when a woman said to me, because a man paid attention to me and not to her, "No matter what, you'll never be
like Heathcliff and Cathy on the moors. You'll never have *that.*"

"No one knows how to shut the windows down on your own
fingers better than you do," one of the most intelligent women
in America, the writer and translator Linda Asher, once said to
me. When we had performed Gardner's play on the stage at the
Studio, Shelley Winters afterward said loudly about my acting,
"She was sent from God." During an audition, Mike Nichols
laughed so hard at my reading that he collapsed over his desk,
couldn't utter the other character's lines anymore. (I just went
on, picking up his part.) But no matter who said or did what on
my behalf as an actress, it was as if I didn't want to be actually
seen moving or talking.

I liked how Nichols laughed, and I still like the blue note in
a blue envelope he sent to me about that audition, out at Para-
mount one afternoon, all those pretty bungalow offices and
trees, and it was good that he told people at the Actors Studio
how good I was, all the serious professional attention. But the
truth is, even right now, I'd rather stay in my room with my
animals and think than take visible action. There is nothing
more fun than thinking in private.

And if you can keep the thinking to yourself, no one beats you up for it. Many years later, George Trow would say, over a Martini at the Waldorf-Astoria, "You needed Jesus, Harold Brodkey, Gardner McKay, and Burt Lancaster to make it through." But at the time, in L.A., Billy the Fish begrudged me the attention of his father's colleagues-at-large in Movietown—a quiet, blond but dark, semi-violent sarcastic hostility, which made it not that hard to retreat. And I did. Often I think of Harold Brodkey later pointing at me and giving the order "Don't retreat!" I had never told him any stories of retreat, but he seemed to know my tendencies.

On and off for a couple of years, I went up to Gardner McKay's house on Coldwater Canyon and typed his journals, short stories, and poems for him (he had his plays typed professionally), while he wrote more of them, in a pleasant, slanted hand. He had an outside patio where there were gray lizards. This he called Lizard Court. It was so nice to sit with him in Lizard Court waiting for a lizard, so nice to be up at his house, being near him, accepting the shelter he offered, laughing and typing with him, a highly stylized younger girl in the old George Koenig, two-against-the-Grocery-People tradition. "Don't look beseechingly," he said once or twice, meaning that there was no cause for worry. He made food for us in his big kitchen: fried eggs, tomato soup.

He had other animals up on Coldwater Canyon: dogs, and wild animals—at one time, two lions, then two cheetahs. When he played with the big animals, it was as if he were a part of them, not a separate, human creature.

There were weeks when I was living with Billy the Fish and retreating from acting when I would take a taxi from Hilldale

up to Gardner's house every single morning. In those days his
brother Hugh said to me, "You and Gardner are like brother
and sister." Gardner would drive me home in the late afternoon,
one or two dogs in his little French car or in an old silver Rolls
that had almost fallen apart. I believe I must have loved him.
And that he loved me back. When he got married, in the mid-
eighties, he brought his Irish bride from Ireland, a painter, over
to my apartment on Sixty-eighth Street, so that we could meet,
so that I wouldn't be altogether left out.

Billy the Fish hated Gardner for being staggeringly Gardner
McKay, and for being well-born (his great-great-grandfather
had invented the clipper ship, and he'd grown up in France and
New York), and mainly because I so evidently loved him. "You
even gave him a nice name," Billy said to me. It was Antelope.
Gardner got the point of everything before I did, I felt, much
the way I knew he would when I lived for watching him in
Adventures in Paradise. One midday when Billy was in the
kitchen of Hilldale having his coffee, Gardner walked in the
back door. I had never before seen two men clash like that,
though both of them kept their good manners. When we got in
his car, Gardner said Hilldale looked like a bowling alley,
because of its long narrow living room. That was the only time
he said anything of the kind (it was the only time he came in).
The rest of the time he referred to Hilldale as the aquarium.

Toward the end of my stay in Los Angeles, Billy went up to his
mother's house, above the Sunset Strip, to stay for a while. I was
by myself in the house on Hilldale, washing my hair and curl-
ing it in the morning with one of those plastic, sit-under-it,
pretend-you're-in-a-beauty-parlor dryers, and then I'd sit on
the ugly sofa, sometimes all day, in a skirt and T-shirt, not reading, not doing anything at all. Sometimes Martine Bartlett, the

actress who had played the schoolteacher in *Splendor in the Grass,* came by to keep me company. Then, in an attack of clarity, I decided to move out of Hilldale entirely, to a place I'd rented when I first moved to L.A.—back to my own baby apartment on Doheny and Sunset, in a pink high-rise apartment house, which I had sublet, so it was still there. I never told Billy I was going to save myself; I just did it. I carried small pieces of furniture, and clothes on hangers, and things in bags, up Sunset to Doheny—I made several trips—in the middle of the night. I saw Billy passing in his blue Volkswagen when I was carrying two yellow kitchen chairs under my arms, but I kept going.

MONIQUE AND THE END OF L.A.

Sometimes a wishy surprise can come out of adultery.
Francine had been living in L.A. for a while when I first
moved there, and one day when she and I were driving
around town in her black M.G.B. we stopped at a little store
with American quilts and antique toys and painted furniture in
it. The owner, a really beautiful man in tennis clothes, had a
French wife, but I didn't know that then. He brought some
quilts to my new pink high-rise apartment on Doheny, and we
had sex in my bed there. He was very refined, didn't say much;
he seemed like perhaps the saddest man I'd met so far. One
night, I was home alone, wearing my best nightgown from
Bendel's, with my hair as clean as if I'd been waiting for someone, and the French wife knocked on the door and announced
herself. Monique. She came in wearing a trenchcoat, and made
some effort to hit me. We ended up calling her husband, he
came over, and we all smoked cigarettes—three little lights in
the dark—and became friends.

Dinners. Driving around. Louis Armstrong records. Ferris
wheel on the Santa Monica Pier. There were thousands of books

in their house—it was like a secret paradise in the middle of a giant trash can—and roses in their garden. After her husband died, in a car crash (he'd written me a note a few days before: "My life is filled with sex and sorrow. I'm going to kill myself tomorrow"), Monique and I remained close. Sisters of the Sacré-Coeur, she called us.

Monique looked more than a little bit like Mick Jagger, except with darker hair and dark eyes, more French—since, of course, she was. When I think of her face, I see it as big, exaggerated, though it was a normal-sized face. She had very full lips decades before very full lips were stylish. Nothing about her looked American, not ever, so if you wanted to pretend you were in France, and eradicate from your consciousness everything cheap and stupid about Southern California, Monique was the one to be around. But that's just one thing. What else she did was make everything and everyone around her look good, in a non–Southern Californian, non-American way. I called this French Pie.

She hated what was *vulgaire* or *ordinaire*. As she put it, *"Je déteste ça."* She dressed me, as if I were a rag doll, in beautiful dresses she had designed and in her own clothes. She taught me how to look like Alison Rose, is what I think now, and even before her husband died they'd made my apartment on Doheny into a pretty baby's room. The house she'd lived in with him and the apartment she later lived in with Gilbert, his best friend, whom she later married, had her parents' furniture from Paris in it and paintings she'd painted, so all that really was French Pie, no two ways about it. But without any French furniture or any paintings she made my room on Doheny look almost as good—"in a way." That's what she would say all the time: "in a way"—a little joke, from Camus, I think.

The getting-dressed-like-a-French-girl lessons were the best times I spent with Monique. I didn't have to be myself from Palo Alto anymore, or myself from New York City, and nothing terrible about Billy the Fish was glued inside my head when I was with her. If she put a plain white Brooks Brothers shirt on my body, she'd pull it this way and that way, kind of yank it out of my skirt and put some of it back in *("Comme ça,* Aleece, *comme ça!")* to make a blouson that I myself couldn't make if I yanked the shirt out this way and that way and put some of it back in. I'd go home to Doheny and Sunset after a lesson, stand in front of my own mirror, put on a similar shirt, yank it out of my skirt, put some back in, but I didn't look French at all, just American with a messy-looking shirt on.

When Monique put a shirt or a dress or any clothes on me, I felt as if she had become my French mother, even though she was only five years older than I. I called her Mamou, and so did other people. She also did this thing with a scarf. The way she wrapped it around my head and tucked and tied it, it looked like a hat. I can feel her folding the silk onto my hair right now. Then, with the scarf-hat on, I felt I was one of those girls in Nice in a Matisse, turquoise shutters in the background, the blue sea.

When we went out grocery shopping, a too bright sun making thought recede, we wore those scarves tied the way she'd tied them on both our heads, low on the forehead. Back in her apartment, she would prepare the food; arrange it, like the scarves, her way. I'd stand around the kitchen, a long narrow one, and wash some lettuce and dry it in one of those plastic baskets where you pull a string. She made *les oeufs* just for me. There was no visible ugliness anywhere.

We didn't talk about food, just liked it and ate it, often on the small balcony overlooking Havenhurst—a view of asphalt, some short apartment buildings. Billy, when he had met her, liked Monique, was ironic about her Frenchness, called her Mon-u-*nique*. The three of us would sit there for hours smoking Kents, more Kents, Camels, Gauloises. Gilbert was there, too, but at an emotional remove. His silence, his very dark hair and darker eyes, had no competition when it came to ravaged dejectedness. Even in photographs, his eyes drifted to the ground. He was American—tall and square-jawed, so that his clothes, arranged in Monique's French way, gave him a further air of separateness.

"Are harmony and beauty depressing?" Monique had said when I first knew her. She often talked about Goethe, Proust, Descartes, and whatnot, as if to solve all the lovesickness and rotten *pensées* in Los Angeles and Europe both. I used to think she did solve these things. I might say, "Billy the Fish doesn't love me and this and that," and she might say, *"Tu es bête,* Aleece, *tu es stupide,* Billy the Fish does love you, and this and that, *mais* that and this," completely reverse everything I'd told her, and then I would be somewhat happy. (She had a goldfish in a bowl she called Bill the Fish, but one night when she was angry— I wasn't there—she threw Bill the Fish against the wall and killed him.)

As much as Monique resembled Mick Jagger, her body was more like Esther Williams's, when Esther Williams was young. I guess it was mainly the shoulders, because Monique used to swim in races in Paris, where she grew up. In between laps in the steamy basement pool of her building, she would pull herself up to the edge of the pool, prop her head on her hands, elbows out to either side, black lashes wet, body underwater, and ask me, "I have wishy legs, don't I, Aleece?" A question. So in this moment she was modest about herself, not all authoritative, more girlish, as if I could have my say, about her legs. Yes, *bien sûr,* they were wishy. *Oui.* Then we were schoolgirls together, asking and answering, and I wished she'd been at the Annie Wright Seminary with me.

Some nights when we stayed at the dinner table talking and talking until the night was almost over, I'd spend what was left of it in the living room on Monique's French-from-Paris day-bed; Porthault sheets, white background with the pink, blue, red *fleurs,* one of the old American quilts, tucked in on either side; tight, *parfait,* which was one of our words. I felt as if I could start my whole life over by pretending this was my first bed, begin again, not be twenty-six, sullen, mopey, downright crazy, *"trop mince,"* as she would say—too thin, Valium-ridden—in Los Angeles.

So when I was all settled there in one of Monique's long Victorian nightgowns, smoking the last Kent of consciousness before blacking out, Monique might come out of their bedroom in a Japanese-kimono robe and say, "Is it *very* baby, Aleece?" And then, *"Vraiment?"* And we'd laugh. It was. *Vraiment.* It was as close as I've ever been to feeling like a real little girl in peace. The daybed felt like a crib, to tell the truth, big and heavy and dark, shelter *extraordinaire* pushed up next to one wall. I could also, sitting up, look out the big windows facing Sunset; all the lights like fake dirty stars, but stars, a dingy brown glow over the unimpressive Hollywood hillside.

I last saw Monique around Christmastime of 1999 in New York City (she was living with Gilbert on Long Island; she died two years later). When I saw her, she had on a dark-blue cashmere coat, longish, with a faint-pink cashmere scarf tucked into the coat in the way only she could tuck things in (*"Comme ça,* Aleece, *comme ça!"*). Her hair was the same; brown, that length to the jaw, and with long bangs. She still had the straightest back a girl could have, a long back, and long legs.

It felt unsettling to see her in New York on a street, but when she came over to my apartment before taking the train back home and I saw her standing in front of the big quilt her first husband had given to me and her drawings on the walls, it all seemed *normale* again. That day she gave me a gold laurel wreath, for Christmas, with small gold berries on it, hammered a nail in the wall, and hung it above the horse that Billy the Fish had made with her blue tissue-paper sky and tinfoil stars in it. Monique was always better than I was at putting nails in walls way high up; not afraid of falling. When you walk in the front door on Sixty-eighth Street, the laurel wreath—it looks like a halo—is what you see first. She could make anything beautiful. She had made me look like French Pie in Los Angeles. When I saw her in New York, I felt *pas normale,* a little, that I didn't try to adjust the clothes or my mind the way she had taught me to. Still, I've "made it through," more or less, anyway, maybe, as she would say, "in a way."

*　*　*

For a long time after I left Hilldale, I sat on my bed on Doheny Drive and smoked. I didn't do anything else. I smoked. In between cigarettes, I had fits of crying about Billy and not feeling alive at the same time. Some nights I went to Monique's for dinner. I wasn't wrong to be sad.

Martine Bartlett would drive over to Doheny in her green Volkswagen and sit in the white rocking chair in one of her long, flowing dresses, smoking Carltons with nervous, shaky fingers. She was around fifty then and nurselike, bringing me groceries and Stouffer's macaroni and cheese—we called them orphan dinners—trying to get me to eat (I was way too thin), and telling me stories about Joe, her family's mynah bird back in St. Louis, where Martine had grown up. I could never hear enough stories about Joe, though now, after thirty years, I can't recall a single one.

We were smoking on the balcony one day when Martine looked down at the people sitting by the swimming pool. "Darlin'," she said, in her *Splendor in the Grass* schoolteacher voice—flat, St. Louis—"that's *Helmut Dantine* down there." She held her breath while her big Midwestern face flushed a real rosy red. "As I live and breathe."

I thought she might pass right out, up there on the eighth-floor balcony, but she didn't. Instead she shook her big, blond, coarse head of hair and said to me in a serious, hushed kind of reverie, "Oh, Sugar, how lucky can you get!"

Helmut Dantine was in *Casablanca,* which I'd watched on television late at night in my bedroom in Palo Alto. He played the downed German pilot in *Mrs. Miniver.* Martine and Gardner and Helmut Dantine had all been on TV in my bedroom in Palo Alto.

Helmut Dantine was living in the building. One afternoon, tired out from smoking and bad thoughts about Billy the Fish, I went down to the pool and sat in the empty green lounge chair right next to the one Helmut Dantine was sitting in. The lounge chairs had been pushed together, side by side, so I was right up close to him. This was a spontaneous act of aggression and self-salvation. "It comes from a kind of death in life," a very smart woman said last summer, having given the subject considerable thought. "You don't get the whole rosebush, but some. The bush loves it, the girl loves it." I love the smart woman for saying that. It's a form of partial reprieve from debilitating sadness. There's nothing like a partial reprieve.

He spoke. I was still thinking of Helmut Dantine in black-and-white, the way he was in those movies, and looked at him now in white tennis shorts and a white button-down shirt by the deep-blue, rectangular Doheny pool with sporty black lines painted on the bottom of it. All this in real-life color. He had beautiful legs. He was a handsome man in an unsettling, not American way. I think he was fifty-nine. The suntan was Southern Californian, but it looked good with his gray hair—he had a lot of it—and dark lashes that fluttered when he stumbled over a word, and brown eyes. His glasses had heavy black rims and thick lenses. He had been, perhaps, reading a script—clean white pages against clean white clothes.

That day, I had managed to get out of my nightgown, wash and dry my hair quickly, and put on navy-blue shorts and a white tank T-shirt, which I thought appeared uncrazy. Monique and I had bought the shorts and the T-shirt on Camden Drive in Beverly Hills, in an attempt to make me look *normale* in the sun, since I refused to wear a bathing suit. Looking that *normale,* I said some more or less engaging sentences about movies. Helmut Dantine had a heavy German accent with a nervous stutter. I paid attention to what he sounded like more than to what he said. There was also silence. When he asked me for my name and telephone number, in his heavy accent, I gave them to him and told him I lived upstairs. Some movie people said Dantine was secretly Jewish. Others said he had spent time in a concentration camp for being anti-Nazi in Vienna, that he had learned how to play a movie Nazi from real Nazis. I never asked him about what people said he'd done or was; it was too upsetting.

After the poolside encounter, he left me telephone messages many times a day. He knew I was sitting on the bed in my apartment, smoking cigarettes, sad about Billy, because I had told him that's what I did up there. "Mr. Dantine called eight times," the woman at the answering service would say, with a swoon. Women of a certain age were jealous that I knew this man, which was immensely amusing, like that Woody Allen movie where the hero walks right out of the movie screen and into real, day-to-day life. Even Monique, who had little interest in movie stars, when I told her I'd come to know him, was startled. "Oh, *Aleece!*" she said. "How did you do *that?*"

George Trow said years later, "Darling, no one understands how you do it, but when you hit *bingo,* you hit *bingo.*" When I was sick of my bed, the cigarettes, and the thoughts about Billy and his blond hair, I went down to the pool to see Helmut Dantine in color, not *Casablanca* black-and-white, no *Mrs. Miniver* Nazi uniform. Just this man reliably all in white by the pool reading his white scripts in the late afternoon. Producing movies was what he did then. He lived in the building because he was getting a divorce.

A few times we went to the movies in his junky American car. His driving made me nervous, but it was a thrill to sit next to his gorgeous face and hard flesh in a normal movie theatre in America. He was a true survivor, though I'm not certain of what, exactly, in the history of the world or his mind. His Second World War presence diminished my Billy the Fish state of emergency. It's surely clear I wanted him in a sexual way, although I couldn't touch anyone after Billy, and didn't, for around eight years.

Some evenings this possibly Jewish man took an elevator ride in his white pajamas up to my apartment. He liked white. He had a little pillow with his wife's first name discreetly embroidered on the white pillowcase, which he brought with him because he liked her. I told him I was unsuited for a human connection and he said in his German accent that this was not true. Definitely not true. He was certain. The way he talked, in a serious voice with specific diction, I believed him for a few days, which was a long time. Helmut Dantine was the only man I called before I left Los Angeles—Gardner McKay was in Europe—because of what he had said about my suitedness for a human connection, and also because he was representing centuries of men in a global way, and gave me the strength to get up and get out of L.A.

Anyway, he's dead now. Mother sent me the newspaper obituary clipping in 1982, all by itself with nothing else in the envelope. Otherwise I wouldn't have known he was dead. I forgot I had told her about Helmut Dantine, but she remembered him, and his face, from movies in the forties. His dark handsomeness was one thing Mother and I agreed about. She had an aversion to blond men.

I moved back to New York. Here's how I did it, and fast:

Monique came over and took down the quilts she and her dead husband had given me. Francine had put them up. Monique packed the quilts expertly in brown moving cartons. One of them that had been hanging over the glass doors, off the balcony, was so sun-damaged we had to throw it away. She packed the clothes; pale-pink pullover, pale-blue one, the navy with the apple on it (the ones we wore as Sisters of the Sacré-Coeur), Raymond Chandler green dress, little hats she'd chosen for me. Scarves. A cold-blooded depression kept me sane while she did this packing, which began in daylight and ended in the dark. When she finished, we took the elevator down and sat in the green lounge chairs by the dark pool under the orange California moon, smoking our Kents.

The movers showed up the next morning and put those yellow chairs I'd carried from Hilldale and all the rest of the stuff, boxes of carefully folded clothes wrapped in tissue paper, down the service elevator and into the moving truck. Those men were going to drive the baby room all the way across the country, as if it were a covered wagon. I didn't take the bed, because Billy the Fish had slept on it with me. After the movers drove away, making a right onto Sunset, Monique and I walked down the block toward Santa Monica Boulevard, where she'd parked her car. "Let's take one last pink look at it, Aleece," Monique said, and that's what we did. We turned around and took a last look. Goodbye, pink high-rise apartment house in Los Angeles.

·   ·   ·

Gillian, a woman my age whom I'd known a little during my first New York days, and who looked like Bette Davis, only taller, with long, enviable calves and ankles, had a one-bedroom penthouse apartment on Seventy-third Street off First Avenue. She was getting a divorce. Before I left Los Angeles, she had agreed over the telephone to let me sleep on the sofa in her living room, an orange-and-yellow floral-print thing with, I found out, dirty tan stuffing coming out in big hunks. During the day, I sat upright on it. Shame kept me on that sofa on Seventy-third Street for a year. I was able to lie down and go to sleep on it at night only because I tired myself out with depression. It's shameful to wonder if you yourself are worth keeping alive. Mother sent two hundred dollars a month for rent and food. I wasn't wrong to go on mourning for Billy. I think that even now.

Gillian stayed in her bedroom nearly all day and night—she read all of Trollope in there—but most mornings she would make coffee, El Pico, come into the living room, and sit in a rocking armchair covered in a zebra fabric that was worn ragged from her sitting on it. Most of the time, she wore a nightgown and a robe, with uncharacteristically unwashed fuzzy pink flat slippers. The zebra chair was right next to the sofa. Neither of us stood up that much of the time. Gillian and I would often laugh ourselves into a delirium with our coffee and cigarettes, just about the absurdity of how we couldn't function and everything else. These laughing times were a spectacular reprieve. Then Gillian went back into her bedroom, shut the door, and read Trollope. I couldn't read a thing.

We did have one visitor, a black woman, Alma, who came in and cleaned once a week. I liked to sit on the green carpet in the hallway and watch Alma scrub the small kitchen floor. I could have done it just as well, Hilldale style, but I didn't clean the kitchen floor, not once. Alma told stories about her family life that made me, and Gillian when I told her, want to go uptown and live there with her.

Some days Gillian and I encouraged each other to just plain go out. I moved one haunch, then the other, slowly, to get up off the sofa. We'd get dressed and go across the street to the Angus Burger for a tuna-fish sandwich and some Greek rice pudding, although, when she felt like it, Gillian was a good cook. There was a blatantly family-like whole roast chicken she made most Saturday nights, with mashed potatoes and peas. It was the one thing I looked forward to. We put the chicken whole onto a silver platter, Gillian carved it, and we ate it at the dining-room table in the living room, like a holiday dinner, except we wore our bathrobes, the wool-challis belted kind with piping. I had charged mine to Mother at Bergdorf Goodman, telling Mother later that the bathrobe was a dress I needed for finding a job.

I had no capacity to do anything except go see Dr. Cederquist, who had moved his office to Central Park South. It was frightening to navigate across town, down Fifth Avenue, and along the Park. I walked, just to see if I could still do that. It was jarring to see the people. Dr. Cederquist didn't think there was anything baffling about the inertia; it was a stern bereftness over Billy the Fish, he agreed. And he knew that, for me, it was the death of a particular vision of Wishiness, and he renewed my prescription for Valium every month. Billy the Fish called now and again. He'd say, "I'm the worst person on earth, Alo," or, "I should be shot."

For a brief period in the winter, Gillian left for Nantucket, to stay with her mother. I lay on the sofa and smoked cigarettes twelve hours a day by myself. Then I slept. That's when the sofa and the stuffing and the zebra chair began to swirl. What swirled more was the bathroom sink, which appeared crooked to my eye, its white porcelain base leaning toward the tile floor. It became difficult to brush my teeth. The safest thing to do was sit on the sofa. Or lie down. Stillness was the point. This crooked-sink phase went on for about two weeks. One late afternoon when I was sitting on the sofa pulling on the stuffing and making it worse, a gray mouse crawled slowly across the bright-green wall-to-wall carpet, rolled over at my feet, and died. Dr. Cederquist said the mouse had been looking for "mammalian warmth."

After the mouse incident, but not because of it, I moved out of Gillian's and went to work for the first time in my life. I can't explain how I did it. A pleasantly humorous, fat man named Jim, whom I'd found in the Yellow Pages, owned an agency for temporary work and had confidence, after he met me, that I could do it. He was a staunch member of Alcoholics Anonymous, and had a large aquarium in his office. All I did then was work, typing temporarily at a hundred and twenty-eight different places, from the dinky kind to Prudential. I was proud to tell Jim every Friday that I had made it through typing insurance forms among strangers and actually liked the days; the waking up at six in the morning in the dark in winter to prepare for these jobs. I liked walking to wherever the job was, the one-hour lunches by myself in coffee shops—the sounds of dishes and cheap silverware crashing. I liked the fact that waitresses called me Honey. My unsuitedness for human connection, or that sensation anyhow, went away. I thought about Helmut Dantine, and we talked from time to time. He had come to the United States when he was nineteen, fifty years before, but his accent still sounded as if he had just stepped off an airplane and rushed to call from a pay phone at LAX, after a longish life spent in Wiesbaden. When I first left L.A., Helmut Dantine said, he didn't sit out there by the pool anymore, because I wasn't there.

In New York, no one in particular meant anything to me, and I lived alone in nice or not-nice places that belonged to other people. A penthouse on Sutton Place had a whole glass wall devoted to the East River, in front of which I'd race back and forth to Rod Stewart's "I Don't Want to Talk About It," fantasizing that I'd already got the job I'd decided I really wanted, at *The New Yorker*. I had made a plan to get myself hired, and, though it took me two years, I carried it out. Then I got my room on Sixty-eighth and I got my cat at the A.S.P.C.A.—a year and a half old, full-grown; I named her Toast—as a reward for not taking any more Valium.

IN ON A PASS

Brendan Gill, a friend of a friend of my mother's, found me the job at *The New Yorker,* where he had been a writer and a singular presence since 1936, when he was twenty-one. I'd called him from Sixty-eighth Street, after I got Toast; and we'd gone for drinks at the Century Club—a grand, formidable New York literary club, at that time solely a men's club. I thought if I met him and got a job at *The New Yorker* I could be a writer somehow, though I barely discussed this with myself. I had defined Brendan Gill as my Last Chance. I couldn't afford one more round of my famous bad judgment, which was, according to my own records at that point, eternal.

When I got to the twentieth floor of the *New Yorker* offices, I found Brendan Gill posing in the corridor in gray and black tweeds, which I was glad of, because it somehow made the clothes I'd chosen to wear—moss-green wool-knit mid-calf skirt, black cashmere pullover, lizard shoes, Monique's tight black wool cloche hat—magically right, and therefore my essence not irrevocably wrong. At the Century Club, in one of the rooms where women were allowed, under a large portrait of

Henry James on one wall, Brendan made wry exchanges with fellow-members who came over to his table and, with dark eyes glancing down at his vermouth, then darting around the room, tossed off descriptions of his *New Yorker* colleagues in enviable, remarkably pretty sentences. He said he was hopping about town nightly because he had "no inner resources." I could have stayed right there all night hearing him talk about *The New Yorker* in the late forties, when editors with proofs of a new Salinger story in their hands strolled down the corridors in a state of editorial euphoria. He recited his favorite first paragraph, from *Tender Is the Night*—"On the pleasant shore of the French Riviera, about half way between Marseilles and the Italian border . . ."—and was still dazzled, as if he were right there in Cap d'Antibes. He said, "I see myself as twenty-six." He was sixty-eight. I asked him if he knew Salinger, and he said, "Jerry's suicidal." I ate bowls of salted nuts and smoked compulsively. The thick-enough gray hair, straight black eyelashes, and the long legs made boyishness at seventy appealing.

I was still wearing my hat, though it was way too hot. I felt bandaged by the hat. He begged me to take the hat off but I refused. "You're hiding your beauty from me," he said. He asked if I was a writer and I told him I had a big cardboard box and that all the papers in the box were about my life in Hollywood; about infatuation, suicide, greed, and blond hair. At the end of the evening (he'd taken me from the Century on to Harry's Bar, in the Helmsley Palace), he said he would find me a job at the magazine. He told me that the editor Rogers E. M. Whitaker had said *The New Yorker* was the place for "congenital unemployables," which sounded promising.

After the evening with Brendan, I had an interview that wasn't quite right. There followed two years of cocktails and

Diet Coke, with Brendan, all around the town. Wherever we were, he made abrupt exits. "I must leap to my feet," he would say, and did just that, and was off, with his long-legged walk and darting eyes, to Grand Central to take a train to Bronxville, where he lived with his wife. They had seven grown children. I went to the *New Yorker* offices fairly often, to see him and to look at the bulletin board for job notices. One day, there was a job for a receptionist listed on an index card. I had an interview with the woman in charge—a gray-haired motherly-looking woman at a desk overlooking a roomful of young things typing. The day before, I had quickly bought a white, button-down Brooks Brothers shirt, so that I might look clean and plain— and fit in, possibly. I wore no makeup. I happened to say to the gray-haired woman that I worried I might be too old (I was almost forty-one), and she said, "Oh, honey, you don't know what old is."

The first morning walking down to my new job—it was June 3, 1985—I wore a long-sleeved white cotton sweater and a longish black linen skirt and black espadrilles. I'd practiced walking it a couple of times to see how long it would take (about twenty-five minutes). I walked down Fifth, by all the green trees in Central Park, and when I got to the statue in the plaza in front of the Plaza—of Pomona, the goddess of abundance, though I didn't know that then—I was reassured to see her. I'd first seen her when I was eighteen, during my first trip to New York, when Mother and I stayed at the Plaza. Over the years, when I've wished for one thing or another, I've stood on the sidewalk by her and looked at her face. What I do is, with the fingers of my left hand I hold the three rings I wear together on the fourth finger of my right hand, the not-married hand, look at her, close my eyes, and wish. When I wished for the job, that came true; others haven't. There was a lot of sun in the sky, an optimism, that start-of-summer thing. Nonetheless I wasn't entirely comfortable about having got what I wanted. I was breaking my own rules.

Before I went to the office, I had breakfast at the Red Flame Coffee Shop, on Forty-fourth Street, where Brendan had taken me a number of times. I sat at what, according to Brendan, used to be Isaac Bashevis Singer's table.

I had poached eggs on whole-wheat toast, for strength.

The New Yorker's offices were three floors in an old midtown building; there wasn't a lot of light in the corridors, which were mostly dusty. When I looked out my sliding glass window onto the elevator lobby of the writers' floor, the whole place was transformed into a big train and I was the conductor. My receptionist's cubicle was very small, maybe six feet by four. Nothing was missing from it that mattered. There was an old pale-green Royal typewriter, the manual kind, a telephone, and a bookcase that had a cupboard with glass doors under two or three open bookshelves, like a china cabinet. Some of the books in the shelves were: *Collected Works of Erasmus #28, Elmer Gantry, The Pushcart Prize: Best of the Small Presses, The Iliad of Homer, The Collected Works of Ralph Waldo Emerson, The Symposium of Plato*. These had all been left by the previous occupant, and I didn't remove them. I supplied *Pale Fire* (my copy from home); later a thin, peach-colored paperback that one of the writers gave to me, called *Are You Stuck?* Nobody ever once talked about any of these books in my cubicle. They were just there, a comfort, which I could count on when I walked in every morning.

The New Yorker didn't remind me of anywhere else I'd ever been. The only real familiarity about it, when I first arrived—

and that was only in my mind—was the air of J. D. Salinger, whose stories I'd first loved decades before at Annie Wright. The stories had nearly all appeared in *The New Yorker,* and here, for me, his Seymour hovered like an invisible spirit, protecting the many people with peculiar ways of thinking.

Around "the magazine," as *The New Yorker* was called by most of those who worked there, it seemed to me at first that the other people who worked there were really "in," whereas I was essentially, irrevocably "out"—as a Californian in New York, no degree from Vassar or anywhere else—and that was one reason my best friend and I ended up calling the place School. Another reason I called it School was that I wrote notes to the boys—long letters, more often than not—and they wrote back. Several of the five men I liked best—Harold Brodkey, George Trow, and three whom I've come to think of as Europe, Personality Plus, and Mr. Normalcy—had been married a few times and were married then. But all of them were—and they made me feel—deeply engaged (*serieux,* Aleece) and seriously attracted. It was affection of another order.

When I wasn't writing notes to these men on my pale-green typewriter, I had to answer the phone, which at least some of the time was deliriously fun, because of other writers who called. "Be brave about your writing," Renata Adler said. "It's better than not." She and I had that kindred thing right away and we still have it. Wives did call, sounding sensible: dinner arrangements, household matters, dentist appointments. Some talked too long, others were terse, one was Portuguese, one had an unrelentingly sad tone in her voice for years: none of them called me by my name, which didn't matter, because I didn't give any of them much thought except when they were on the other end of the telephone line, because the eighteenth floor was *mine*.

.   .   .

I answered the telephone in my cubicle with the words "Eigh-teen floor." Wallace Shawn, the editor's son—the innest of the in, and also a writer, though not for School—would say to me "Hello, Eighteen" when he called up. He said it in the most approving way. One time I ran into him out in the world, near the Plaza Hotel, and he waved madly, and shouted over half a New York City block, as if across a mountainside, his baby voice forceful, "Eighteen! Hello!" He had a semi-fake name for himself, too: Wall, as if he were a secret agent. He called me Eighteen in a way that showed he understood that a person in this small prison-cubicle would of course have her own reasons for having a job like this. Maybe something unmentionable. The five men understood this, too. The eighteenth floor was the main writers' floor, and at that magazine writers were a tribe of gods.

Everybody thought so.

"The idea of you losing your looks is ludicrous," Harold Brod-key said to me, standing in the doorway of my cubicle on the eighteenth floor—tall, large, a sizable Hunting World bag over his shoulder, and with an unalterable seriousness on his whole face. Then he said, "I know I'm attacking you with this. But you're so pretty it doesn't matter. And anyway I'm going to commit suicide soon." And then, "Aren't you glad you know me?"

I was.

Harold would tell everyone at this new place that I was really smart. He would do it in the corridor. He'd say, "Isn't she pretty?" and "She's really smart," in an exaggerated Harvard accent, and it sounded as though he were reading the Bible out loud. If I seemed downtrodden some morning, he might charge around from the lobby in his long coat, lean in the doorway, and say, "Take up your position as countess," or, one time, "Write a column from a femme semi-fatale."

When he said these things, I would straighten my back, sit up very straight in my chair, as if at attention, and not say anything. If I'd said anything, it would have taken us on a different track, and I wanted to keep what he'd said and what it felt like to me in my mind for as long as I could. It was like holding my breath.

I loved the way he smoked, as if the cigarette mattered to him as much as writing did. He said he smoked to make himself sit still. If Harold was smoking, I liked to smoke with him, so I'd light one of my Kents quickly with a green plastic lighter I had on my desk. We'd smoke and I would quote lines of his writing to him and it was just him and me in that little cell, all smoky. I never answered the phone at those times, and when people had to be buzzed in they would pick up their yellow message slips from my desk fast and shut my door again, to convey that they had been intruding. If Harold thought I was smart, I thought so, too. If he said I was pretty, I was pretty—pretty and smart, at least when he was saying it. What his face looked like when he said these things, as if he liked me, was all I cared about.

One day, after eating a fat turkey sandwich on white toast with mustard (I'd ordered it for him), he was sitting in my other chair, in black jeans and a gray T-shirt—his shoulders looked so good in it—and said something I liked better than anything else he ever said. "Normalcy is very useful—it's a form of looks, only safer." He said it as if offering me the greatest salvation that could ever come my way. He was generous that way all the time. Whatever the thought that had partially rescued him, he handed it over, so that I'd be partially rescued, too. "Build a life out of bad judgment," he said another time. Then he added, "*I* have." I wrote this down, took it home, and taped it to my refrigerator, where it's been ever since. After a few years, it looked so old and tattered I copied it over on a fresh piece of paper, imitating my handwriting from the day I first wrote it down. Some of the best things anyone's ever said to me were said in, or in the doorway of, my cubicle at School, which was *The New Yorker* magazine in the mid-eighties.

. . .

Mornings at School would go like this: Penelope Gilliatt—one of the few women who used to visit me in my cubicle—would lean into my doorway. Penelope had thick bright-red hair that flipped at her shoulders or was swept back into a French twist; a long, straight, pointed nose; and a good figure. She got all dressed up every single day—silky blouses with frills, under dressy suits—and wore extremely high thin heels. She was from England, and smart—so smart she may have been smarter than any of the men there, and once when I said that to a couple of them no one argued about it. One morning she said, as if she understood the very essence of my mornings at home preparing for School, "*Dar*-ling! Freshly washed *American* hair!"

Penelope writes out the title of her latest novel for me. She tries it different ways. Yellow message paper and black felt-tip pen. We talk about the possibilities, about the "graphics." I'm nervous that what I'm saying isn't good enough, helpful, so I try to be funny. George passes by. "It's wit corner," he says. Penelope and I giggle. "This is the place to be," he goes on, "where the girls talk fast." This is our cue for laughter. We laugh. George goes out the door and down in the elevator. I tell Penelope I think I look like a baboon. She understands I'm in some way serious. She makes a drawing of a baboon, then one of me. I do see the difference, according to her.

I still have her drawing of the baboon and me, and all the notes and other drawings she left on my desk. On a yellow message slip Penelope made me a drawing of Toast, in my front window, waiting for me to come home from School. There is the window, the windowsill, Toast, and, next to her, a vase with flowers in it. Under this drawing Penelope wrote Toast's words: "She's coming soon and I'll see her a lot because it's Friday and then Saturday, and then Sunday." Coming onto the paper from the bottom is another drawing, of the back of Toast's head, and, beside that, "GETTING NEARER EVERY MINUTE."

Penelope's notes were like presents waiting for me in the mornings. At School, I did have momentary regressions into ancient feelings of freakishness, but after I read her notes the feelings went away.

Alison—
I shall be in the office tomorrow and Wednesday except for fragments of outness that resist attempts to time them.

Once she described me, in my circumstances, as "guilty with explanation."

A lot of the time, when I was listening to my visitors or typing or reading, I didn't push the buzzer button fast enough.

This made people waiting to get in the lobby door furious, and I was sorry they were furious, but it was hard to listen hard and pay attention at the same time. I mean, if I was listening to something Harold or someone was saying, and was nervous they were going to leave my cubicle any second, because they had the freedom to do that, then some kind of panic or fury took over and I just plain didn't see the person waiting exasperatedly to get in. Most of the time I was forgiven. Jonathan Schell, a serious, polite, blond, and highly respected man who wrote about the state of the world for School, told me he'd advise the people in charge that I needed a new window—one that opened more easily to receive packages—and a new buzzer system, so I wouldn't have to be interrupted when I could be reading and writing.

Every single Monday, someone came around distributing the "rough copies"—they had the word "ROUGH" stamped somewhere on the cover, and were the first copies printed of each week's issue. There was nothing like opening up a rough copy and reading a piece by someone I'd just seen wandering around the corridor. I did not, at that time, have any understanding of how the magazine actually came out every week. The eighteenth floor was a cool backwater (only one editor had an office on eighteen), and I was almost completely disconnected from the people who made the place exist and be what Liz Macklin—a query editor, and another woman who visited me, coming down from nineteen—called "a working magazine."

Because it was a working magazine, most of the time I was, of course, alone in my cubicle, no men or anyone else around. It was usually quiet, writers maybe wandering out of their offices with galleys in their hands, or, once in a while, when two or three of the professionally funniest of them would gather in one office, laughing raucously, shrieking and squealing like maniacal children, and then they'd come out of the office and tell me what was so funny, all of them talking and laughing at once. When it was quiet, I would type and type on my green typewriter, sometimes saying nonsense things out loud to myself, like "So furry!" or "Chicken and rice!"

One writer, from his office nearby, would hear me say these things, and like an echo I'd hear "So furry!" or "Chicken and rice!" from over there. I'd keep on typing.

I wrote letters to Europe every day. Europe had big hands and fluffy hair, and the most beautiful clothes; his shoes were so soft I imagined you couldn't find them ready-made in a store. Europe had better manners than the other men and always said the right thing to everyone, though often with a slight stammer. He had written a contagiously glorious book about his life. In a lot of ways, reading it made you want to have his life instead of your own. He called my letters "bulletins" and would stand in my doorway, looking expensive and slightly forlorn, waiting for me to hand over a bulletin.

When I wasn't writing letters, I would read. Since I'd read almost everything of Harold's before I met him, it was just about entirely impossible that I wouldn't become attached to him when he came to have an office at School. Harold seemed to like me better than anybody had so far in my life. On a yellow piece of message paper he wrote one day, in pencil, "What an admirably dark person *you* are." Above the handwriting is a dime—paying me for a letter—with a long piece of Scotch tape over it. Mostly I read old issues or bound copies of the magazine, with all the stories that Europe and Harold and George Trow had written over thirty years. When I first met Harold, I told him how I lived and breathed for reading his sentences—I think I actually said exactly that. He wrote sentences like "People don't like to be outshone. They'll kill you if it bothers them enough." The way he said things gave me all the legitimacy I needed, and more. That's one reason he called me My Bride. Another of his names for me was Already Utterly Ruined. Our anxieties and our varying degrees of murderousness were a common ground.

"Another moral universe," George Trow said once about School, sitting in my other chair. He also said, perhaps referring to the outside world, perhaps not, "Self-aggrandizement and persecution are so hard to live with without a break."

"I do understand," I said.

"You're mentally tough. That's what keeps us going, saves us."

He sighed, deeply, as if letting all of himself out of himself. (He did that often.)

George at some point told me that William Shawn, the head of the whole School—the editor-in-chief—had strongly suggested, years before, that Harold and George meet, and they did. Years later, a few months after I got there, Harold, in something of the same manner, told me he thought it was important that George and I "meet."

This was my account of our first meeting:

George is a new twisted thrill, a blond one. I caught him eating porridge in the window of The Fountain this morning. He wanted to be caught, I guess. But with a sad little fried egg approaching? I saw the strawberry jam through the glass, spy-like. Then I got up my nerve and went in. "About last night," George said, "you should be *ashamed*." "I'm never ashamed. That's my sickness," I said. He had a way of chewing his food that was vehement, and he did that. I left the coffee shop.

George wrote stories that were funny and essays that a lot of people thought were important. Some other people couldn't understand a word of what he wrote. "He's so brilliant no one knows what he's talking about." A friend of mine told me Elizabeth Hardwick had said that. I once asked George's father what he thought about George's brilliance. "Oh," he said, shaking his head, "I could never get anywhere near it." But the best thing about George to me was the way in conversation he said one thing and then another that wasn't connected to it. He was always thinking behind his own back while he was thinking. He had so many thoughts you had to listen very hard. "I don't tell you very much, but I don't keep anything from you," he said one time, sitting in the other chair and making blond twine of a piece of his hair. He used his hands a lot when he was talking, particularly when he was being especially droll: they looked awkward when he threw them around in the air and pointed and squinted at the same time. When he finished the hair-twirling, I knew it was a warning that he was going to get up and walk away very fast in his big shoes. I knew everyone's footsteps, and George's were heavy; he always wore big shoes, like a workman—carpenter's shoes.

. . .

Mornings at home getting dressed, getting ready to see them all again—that was another thing I liked. I liked to put on a Louis Armstrong tape, eat Grape-Nuts, and have coffee sitting up in bed, my back against the wall. I might have a dialogue with George in my head, make myself laugh, just tell him my thoughts about absolutely anything. I would imagine him sitting in my room, wearing an old white shirt with creases in it, arms folded, feet on the floor, shouting and talking and laughing, just as he did at School; a liveliness so fierce it seemed possible he would wear himself out. Or, after I had washed and dried my hair, and put on my black skirt and one of the sweaters I wore all the time, I might sit in a chair in front of the full-length mirror on the inside of one of my open closet doors, and smoke a cigarette with myself, maybe two. I would try to figure out what they saw—all the other men—when they had conversations with me in my cubicle. I mean, I was wearing the same clothes and smoking the same cigarettes, and crossing my legs the same way, and since I was thinking about them very hard, I thought that maybe that's what my face looked like when they talked to me at School. I saw my concentration and some smoke in the reflection. I don't think I was wrong to imagine that I made them say things they wouldn't have said if I hadn't been, I admit it, starry-eyed, excited to hear what they'd say next, often astonished by the attention, and intent on charming them if I could. When George Trow, after some months, said to me, *"Darling. We don't smoke,"* I stopped the next day and have not had a cigarette since.

In the late mornings and in the afternoons, someone from the Typing Pool would come downstairs to sit at my desk for twenty minutes. Eventually, these breaks turned into a half hour and longer; the people who filled in for me liked it in the cubicle, too. When I was set free, I would take the autonomy I had in the cubicle and go visiting, which was perhaps the best fun of the whole day. The office doors were mostly closed, and my espadrilles quiet on the linoleum. Sometimes I could get so excited I would literally run to see Harold, and I didn't care if people saw me running and gave a disapproving look. His demeanor would be different outside my cubicle; he seemed more shy, also, as if he were under siege. In his own office, he couldn't say just one perfectly composed, noble sentence and walk away—none of them could do that when I visited.

Despite this particular nervousness of his, to me the visits seemed more physically comfortable: just me talking to a man, not a man stealing a few minutes, saying something witty while my distracting old telephone rang. What was really fun was when I would hand over a letter I had written for one of them, and he'd read it while I was sitting in his office. What their faces looked like when they read the letters was better than any other attentiveness I had had before then, or any that I've had since. Sometimes I'd stay away from the cubicle far too long, making my replacement a little annoyed, but not too much. Whatever "Take up your position as countess" had meant exactly when Harold said it, I'd pretty much done that.

Another way to spend the break was to sit on one of two worn couches in a niche of the corridor, a wide spot in the main thoroughfare on eighteen, around two corners from my cubicle. Most people were in their offices, concentrating on their work. The sofas were inappropriate to the setting, like a living room in a desert. I might read on one of the hallway sofas. Someone walking by might stop, say something ("I *am* weird, and there's nothing I can do about it"), and go on walking. Penelope usually kept her nearby door open and would hear people chatting and laughing, and come out—and then these "gods" would outwit one another. They'd talk about the Theory of Something or Another, as opposed to some other theory, and make a parody out of it. Penelope might bring up music or math, and knock George, say, out of the water. The camaraderie—one person's pleasure in the other's mind, regardless of subject matter— was a comfort to me. I would just listen and hold on to the time for as long as I could without getting into too much trouble. Then I'd have to literally run down the corridor back to my job.

Sometimes some of us would sit on the couches in the evening. One night Harold, lying down on one of the sofas, said right in front of Penelope, "Women want to kill me." "No, they don't, Harold," I said, and Penelope commented, "But that's the way he feels." I was sitting next to his head, and I could see his legitimately dazed expression, upside down, when I said, "What I want is to kill other people when I sense they want to kill you." At that point, he said our cahoots were "eternal," now, without any sort-ofs or maybes. He said that right in front of Penelope. After that, Penelope and I took a taxi uptown.

．　．　．

Sometimes in the mornings George would walk in on the eighteenth floor, look at me while standing in my doorway, and then, with impeccable timing, heavily flop into the famous other chair and invent something giddily out-on-the-town—one time it was "I would have come back last night to say I'm sorry, but I went to Dazzles instead." That time, he asked me for a kiss. So, with only the smallest hesitation, I kissed him on the cheek. It felt like a regular man's cheek—instead of a thinking machine's. George said his day would have been "ruined" without it. One time he called in sick from his house upstate, and I asked him, "Is it fun to be sick in the country?" What he said, in a sullenly confessional but sly tone of voice, was "You always know what I'm not really saying." When I asked if he had a pretty bathrobe to be sick in, he said no. There was a silence, sort of long, and then he said, energetically businesslike, "Next time I'm in New York I'm going to take you with me at *gun*point to buy a *bath*robe!"

. . .

Again and again, whenever he was in my cubicle and we were talking, George would say, as if he were training a big guard dog for police work, *"Darling: Write that down."* Then he'd point to a piece of yellow message paper with so much force in his pointing index finger, and his eyes narrowing a little bit, that I'd write whatever it was down, fast, because I was nervous and also because the point was not to lose it. The main thing at the time was that he'd understood what I meant and agreed with it and he ordered me to write it down.

Sometimes, when lots of men stopped by at once, and when it was possible—the phone not ringing too much—I'd write down what each one of them said, in a big hurry:

"I don't want a fanciful answer, I want the facts." (One of the cartoonists, mock furiously: I hadn't seen him at the door, didn't buzz him in, he had to use his key.)

"This is Alison. Our resident heartthrob."

"I get my strength from her."

"Being out of trouble makes you a little sad."

"Life is endless."

"People are always gathered in here around you. That's not company."

"You looked so pleased with what you were writing, I didn't want to rap on the window."

"I see you in white tennis shorts—*The Garden of the Finzi-Continis.*"

"Harold and Alison are in deep cahoots." George said that.

"A sweet disposition counts, too."

Often one of these men would say a sentence that was as good as anything they wrote. Harold to me, smiling a characteristic smirk of his: "Persevere, persist, severe sister." Another: "Sanity means hard work and a view of life not so droll." My favorite sentence that George ever said out loud in my presence was this: "Darling, we're in on a pass." He meant that others were here in some normal way but that we—he and I—were on leave together, in town on a pass, as if from our submarine in some alternative harbor, and that the pass might not last much longer. It identified my circumstances exactly. "Ordinary human contact," he said another time, meaning we didn't have much of that. "We don't have *all* the magic on our side." But I still think we did, for a while.

When I'd been there a few years, George and I formed a club, which he decided to call Insane Anonymous. We were the only members. When something nice happened—a trip we took to a small beach on the Hudson, maybe, or Toast not dying when she got sick—he would say, in a radio broadcaster's voice, as if explaining a stay of execution, "I.A.: a miracle grant from the I.A. Foundation."

That was School.

. . .

Most of what I wrote down of what people said to me was, of course, flattery. The flattering things seemed *true* when these people said them. Europe said a flattering thing that I've had on my refrigerator (on faded yellow message paper) ever since the day he said it: "A beguiling person such as you; the boring people, it's unsexy." Of course, there were different kinds of flattery. George said, "Nothing bad will ever happen to you again," which was a lie, but at the time he meant that he was in charge and I was safe.

I liked to remember the compliments and reassurance the way some people remember what certain philosophers have written, to combat enemy thinking or actions. (George one time said this: "It's amazing how many invitations people give you to be weak," which is completely true.) For nearly four decades, enemy thinking, as I'd experienced it, was people deciding that the way I saw things was punishable by exile. Enemy-thinking people seemed to have a ceaseless, brutal active desire to punish; perhaps it made them feel superior and powerful. The writers at this School, who in their context were superior and powerful, were a divine present to me—their ease, which created a freedom from worrying about enemy thinking. The destruction it had done to me so far, like my conviction that I just plain didn't belong in the world, was gone, or it felt like it.

"*Dar*ling," Penelope said to me one day, "you're lenitive and droll," and continued tottering down the corridor in those high-heeled pumps. I looked up "lenitive" in the dictionary and it said: "alleviating pain or harshness, soothing." No one had ever called me anything like that before.

* * *

"You have to have a machine gun in your heart," George announced to me one day. I never asked him for advice, I just got it. I had never seen George when he was a young man, when he had all his blond hair; but a very gentle older woman who had worked in Accounting for years and years stopped me in the hallway and spoke softly about how handsome George had been when he was young, in his twenties. She described him all dressed up, as if in a white dress uniform and with his blue eyes all lit up the way they often were. While she was describing him, she shook her head and looked down at the linoleum, as if she were talking about a husband she'd lost at sea many years before. This was at the height of my relationship with George—what we would come to call Trow-Rose—and that's why she stopped me to talk. I could tell she still loved something about him and had wanted to tell someone. Not long after, I ran into her in front of Saks and I made her tell me about the blond hair and the white uniform all over again. I liked to think of him that way.

. . .

I had two wrist incidents with Harold. The first happened one afternoon when he said, with the trace of a smirk, "I never forget about you, Alison," then got up and, standing over my desk in black jeans and turtleneck, wrote his name on the inside of my left wrist with green ink, like a tattoo.

The second took place a half year later, the week before Christmas, when we'd had an argument and he'd walked away. He was back in a few minutes, to show me an inch-long scratch on the inside of his wrist, red but not bleeding. I didn't ask him how he got it.

"This is your fault," he said. "If you cry again I won't be able to do any work." He extended his right hand, the one without the scratch above it, for me to shake, and I shook it, as if we'd made a deal.

One day when Harold was away, Dan Menaker, a fiction editor, stopped by and asked me for a Kent. "Heard from Harvey?" he said, meaning Harold. And then, to make it worse, though perhaps he didn't mean to, "Heard from Hank?" I tried to answer nicely and I gave him a Kent.

"Since Harold's gone, why not throw a little attention my way?" George asked me that same week.

"I thought you might find it repellent," I said.

"Not as long as you keep coming up with those snappy answers."

Going down in the elevator with me later, Chip McGrath, an editor of both fiction and fact, said, "How are you getting along without Harold?" "I have George," I said, lying. "Harold's alter ego," he said. We looked at our feet.

Then he said—out of the blue, for him, and as if to justify my whole life—"You see beyond."

Harold was sometimes competitive: he was actually a little obsessive about the tallness competition (six-two to six-four) with another one of the writers, which he couldn't win. And one day he did say, "I want to look like [Europe] for two weeks." Harold said he liked my pink lipstick; George liked the red. "It's a petite war," I wrote to Europe. "I am so amused that they have given the matter some thought."

I told Europe and Harold and George a lot about Mother.
Bulletin to Europe:

A package from Mother is delivered to my desk on eighteen. Harold stands there while I open it: He knows I'm afraid of the package, because it's from Mother. "I'll stand here while you open it," he says.

That first summer at School, I wrote a few paragraphs for Harold about Mother and how, when I was six, I made a small bed of clay for her and glazed it pink. A little strip of clay, a narrow one, against the backboard of this bed, had represented Mother sitting up in bed, in one of her pink bed jackets. Harold said to write more of those paragraphs and then it would be "a real story." He said he'd "see to it," "make changes in the margins." Harold understood everything about the ways Mother made me hideously nervous. I wrote him a long letter—I was on my way to Atherton—about how I'd gone to Bergdorf Goodman at lunchtime to buy a new nightgown Mother couldn't see through, a thicker cotton. She was intrusive about those physical things. He understood that. *All* of it. The next day at a French restaurant, George said, "Is there anything you like about your mother? Her skin? Her hair?" After that he declared, "Everything is really very nice. Really very nice, and you want to know why?"

He held his knife up, and answered himself: *"Because there isn't any alternative."* Then he put some more butter on his bread. He always ate a lot of bread and butter in a restaurant. I loved the way he used his knife, putting it down on the tablecloth with a thud after he'd used it to butter the bread. This is part of what I would mean if I said he was optimistic.

Harold said "love" was the forbidden word between us. In a moment of really not caring what anyone might think, I wrote down Harold's name on the personnel department's emergency-contact If I Should Die form. George, sitting in my other chair, was my witness. If death was to be an extension of an absurd existence, I told him, I should have the right name on my certificate, at least insofar as School was concerned. I was kind of sad it wasn't Europe on the little piece of paper.

"My Bride," Harold calls to me in the corridor.

"My Conscience," I answer.

When I'd told Harold I was going to visit my mother in Atherton, he got upset. He was at the bend in the hall, and I was outside my cubicle, in the middle of the corridor. His voice was never as loud as George's, but now it was loud, for him, and he kind of yelled, "My Bride, *how long will you be gone?*"

"My Conscience, I'll be back the twenty-second," I answered.

He yelled, with a certain odd whisperiness inside the yelling, "*That doesn't mean anything to me.*" And then, really yelling, "HOW MANY DAYS?"

Harold called me from home, as he often did in the mornings at School. He said, "I came to see you yesterday. I knew you had to see me before you went to California, but you weren't there."

"But I don't go until next Thursday," I said.

"Oh," he said. "I'm so mixed up."

I didn't have to *ask* Harold to visit me before I visited Mother and failed to become Miss Jones. He just knew he had to; a matter of life and death.

"Don't say anything. Just be here next time I'm hungry," Harold said as he left one Friday. We'd had lunch, picnic style, in his office. He was using Jane Kramer's office, northern light, and it had a daybed as a park bench. "I wanted you to fall in love with me so you'd do things for me," he added. Harold brought me, in my cubicle another day, a peanut-butter sandwich in the form of two saltines dyed orange and pasted together with peanut butter. I ate it while he sat and watched. I said I liked his shirt. He said he'd give it to me. I said I wanted it now. He said later was better. (I wrote in a bulletin to Europe, "Harold has his limits, has more discipline than I do.")

Harold loved his wife, and he claimed that she had said, "I'd rather you had an affair than smoke." ("She wants you alive, not dead," I said to him.) We smoked. He said having an affair with me wasn't a good idea anyhow, because I was "undefended." He did say one time that if I married George, *then* he and I could have an affair, though I knew he wasn't serious.

But: "Someone who halfway understands—it's tempting," Harold had said. "I played verbal tennis with Renata for twenty years." And he said, "I can get serious, too."

ALISON: It's hard for me to be serious.
HAROLD: I figured that. You know what I like best?
Breaking your heart.
ALISON: I have this impulse to embrace you.
HAROLD: It's too dangerous. (*Pause.*) I have an impulse to embrace you, too, but I ignore it. Only when you get really ugly.

I wrote him a series of way too hysterical love letters.

ALISON: Here's a love letter. It's not too bad.
HAROLD: You always say that. But they always are. Now, I've told you: *not until you lose your looks.*
ALISON: They're gone.
HAROLD: No, they aren't. Go away, now.

Harold and I on the street, in the dark, outside School, in winter, as he was on his way to the Four Seasons, continuing the discussion about the "affair" we continued not to have:

HAROLD: This is farewell for now. (*Alison stands there, doesn't move.*) I'll ruin your life.
ALISON: I've already done that.
HAROLD: I'll make it worse.

In his office one day, I told him I'd framed his bird drawings (including the "Wow! A Happy Ending" one). He said his wife hadn't framed any. I said, "She doesn't need a souvenir to remember you—"

"—by," Harold said.

Another day I'd given him flowers, heathery-looking things from the florist across the street on Forty-third, to say I was sorry for getting upset the day before. I had called him from a phone booth in what I referred to, in the note, as "a burdensome fit of emergency."

A moment of embarrassment and avoidance before the flowers. Then "What should I do with them?"

"Should I have hysterics, or should I control myself?" I asked Harold the day before another departure—I forget now where he had been going off to.

"Control yourself, because I get hysterical, too," he said. He went on, "We've had fights about emergencies since we've known each other. I can only handle your emergencies when I don't have one of my own. Otherwise, I have to wonder how you are for fifteen minutes, and I can't do that when I'm crazy. Now, listen, you're strong as an ox." I wrote it down right in front of him. He'd said long before, "You're my recording angel."

I gave Harold a gray cashmere scarf I'd charged to Mother at Bergdorf Goodman. My note read: "John Keats, John Keats, John. Please put your scarf on" (quoted from Salinger). He started to cry and told me he had to go buy a doll for his granddaughter. I started to cry, too. There was black mascara all over my face.

"What's wrong with you?" a young writer said after Harold had left.

"Harold's gone," I said.

"Not forever," he said.

"In a way," I said.

When Harold called the next day, he said, "My wife's letting me keep the scarf." I told him about the young writer and the mascara, and he asked me if I was O.K.: "I don't want to talk seriously because it turns you on," he added.

"I have control over myself."

"No, you don't."

Then he said, "Is this thing eternal?"

I said, "Very eternal."

He said he would see me the next Monday, and that I'd survive until then. And what I thought was this: If I have, say, twenty fragments of my mind all to myself, and I give ten to Harold, then half of them are taken care of for a few hours. Then I only have half the trouble, half the isolation. A real luxury.

I saw Harold go out the door on another such occasion, leaving on another trip. He was standing in front of my cubicle window, but facing the elevators, and it was awful. There were some women out in the corridor, office talk going on: which office, something about offices. The women disappeared. Then Harold came up to the window and I opened the little sliding partition. He offered his hand. I put my hand through the very small opening in the window, and we touched fingers.

"Infidelity, that's how it begins," he said slowly.

He went to push the elevator button.

"I'm in jail," I said loudly, so he could hear me out there.

"We all are," he said.

"ALL OF US WHO LOVE YOU ARE YOUR COVER"

Outside School, the man I liked the best in these years was a man I didn't get to know very well. I knew him for about a year. His face always looked as if his thoughts were connected to sex. He couldn't help it. He was a rock-and-roll icon, actually did that for a living. Around other people it was disconcerting to think about his face or to see it. It was just his physiology, really, along with his face: he liked sex, real sexual sex.

He didn't like sex only because he was depressed, though he did suffer from a near-fatal depression. He simply wasn't nervous about sex. He loved it, and not because he wanted to do it in some particularly original way. Rather, he put his whole entire body into sex and, having sex with me, made me feel, in a physical way anyhow, that I was a living thing.

We never said anything at all in bed. I liked to look at his eyelashes, when he closed his eyes. There was no futility war in my head when I was with this man. His darkness—which was as Jewish as he was—made me a part of the darkness of all other

Jews from all centuries. Or maybe the nonfutility was because he showed he was very, very attracted to me, showed it to the point where I believed him. I also liked his shoulders: he had bones that showed. I also liked his neck, which was somewhat thick. His skin was not smooth, which was good—ungirlish. He wasn't married at all.

I'd met him in Bemelmans Bar at the Carlyle Hotel, at a small table, when he was talking with a friend of his whom I'd come there to meet for drinks. Even as he was introduced, he was one of those presents from the sky, destabilizing, dazzlingly unexpected, like Billy when he showed up in the large brown house on Beverly Drive. I sat down at the table, Ludwig Bemelmans' drawings of dogs all over the walls behind it, and looked at the sexily dejected face this man had. I was kind of immobilized by it. My friend and this man were already having drinks when I was introduced to him; I ordered my Diet Coke with lemon, and in the middle of it and the salty potato chips he said, "You're so pretty I just can't take it," and soon after that got up and left, in a way that was abrupt and rude to our mutual friend.

One night on the sidewalk at the corner of Sixty-eighth Street when he and I got out of a taxi—he'd called me at School after that first meeting—he put his hands under my black cardigan sweater and wrapped them around my back. It was as if he couldn't help it, sort of like a fit. When he did this, the door of the taxi still open, the driver waiting, I said, "I'm almost like a normal person," and he said, both hands still under the black sweater and on my back, "Exactly like a normal person." We started to laugh. And he held me up close to him with more force than anybody ever had on a street corner. Then he got back into the taxi, went uptown, and I crossed the street and went home.

He had a full, melodica player's mouth and big eyebrows, and a look on his face as if he'd nearly given up on life but had retrieved himself, though he remained startled by the rescue. I think about his face being like that when I want a good reason not to shoot myself, or just to cheer up.

Almost as sexy as sex with him—not quite, but almost—was going to the movies with him. It really was immensely difficult to sit next to him through any movie, because of the unhealable attraction; I listened to the way he breathed in the movie theatre, an unease in the dark. He held my hand in a tough way, hard.

In my room, on top of my bed, he played a game with Puppy Jane called Catch and Press. He made it up, as far as I know. He would gesture toward her, call her; she'd back off. They'd do that a few times, and then he would say, "Catch," and would catch her. He'd put both hands on either side of her rib cage, she'd make small fretting motions; then he'd press, very, very gently, on either side, Puppy white in his hands, and he'd say, "Press," and she'd be still. That was Catch and Press. Puppy Jane liked to play it over and over again.

Even now I like thinking of his face when he played with Puppy Jane, because it was serious with a different seriousness from his seriousness when we were in bed. I could see she felt an unusual energy inside him there in bed, on the white top sheet with its blue scallop hem. He said to me once, "I stole your incredible lightness"; but the energy I took from him was a dark thing. A darkness so dark I wanted to stay in it and didn't miss blond, or anybody, at all.

·   ·   ·

Mr. Normalcy's expression was almost as sulky and satirical as my rock-and-roll singer's, but I saw him every day at School.

He was younger than I was, and a more normal kind of man, not to mention married. Our School-day call and response of "Chicken and rice!" and "So furry!" aside, he overdid it with the semi-faux conventionality, so much so that Harold once dared him to write a book about normalcy. He should have done it.

He had a good amount of all-American bulk. His whole body was bulky, though not at all fat. It was the kind of body one could imagine hurling oneself against and feeling sudden insulation from outside blows. He said he was six feet tall. He had dirty-blond, slightly wavy hair, unremarkable blue eyes, and a robust laugh, which wasn't fake. He liked nonsense, and found his own raucously amusing, which was fair, because he was, at the very least, funny. Every single day. And yet he was so normal that I could introduce him to my mother when she came to town, and I did that one evening, at Bemelmans Bar.

The man playing the piano and singing—"all those charms in one man's arms makes you easy to dance with"—was too noisy for Mother. Even so, she talked about the drawings of the dogs on the walls, and Mr. Normalcy told her—in a voice more firm and louder than his usual boylike voice, straining over drinks and potato chips—what a good writer I was, what devoted friends I had at School, that she should be proud of me. She liked him more than any other man I'd introduced her to, and for a while they sent witty notes to each other across the country.

There was a song I had started singing to Toast at home. Whenever I sang it in my cubicle, it made Mr. Normalcy laugh. I didn't think it up on purpose, it was just there.

Whip a kitty, thrash a kitty
Whip a kitty, twice

Whip a kitty, thrash a kitty
Whip a kitty wi' chicken and rice.

He had become a fan of Toast's early on, sending her cards with frequency, insisting daily that I remind Toast that he was her "constant friend." The intimacy of routine was maybe the best thing about School.

He gave me some nice gray shorts for my birthday one year, and I bought him a raincoat that he wore for years. I sometimes called him for reassurance when I felt depressed. He did come over to my apartment, but not that often. Sometimes on his way in or out at School he would grab me, my whole self, hard, and kiss me on the lips in the cubicle and then run away fast, so he wouldn't get caught. One time, he said I was pretty as if there were no two ways about it. "But what about when I get old?" I asked. He said, "You're old now," which was true, so that remark oddly gave me confidence.

He could be humanitarian in an irritating way. Once, two polar bears killed a little boy at the Prospect Park Zoo, in Brooklyn, and the authorities shot them. I was upset that the bears had died (I have a rule about No Dead Animal Stories), and when I told him that he said, "You're a twisted person," and added, "I want to fuck you, but I don't like you. You have no humanity." Somehow I didn't say, "Fuck you, too." I didn't want to lose him.

Another time, though, I remember his being humanitarian toward me. We were in his Volvo going up Madison, and he said I was the only person who knew he wasn't really normal. "Without my wife and kids, I'd be a first-rate lunatic," he said. "They're my cover." There was a small pause. I said, "But I don't have a cover." He parked his car in front of my building, switched off the ignition, turned to face me, and said, "All of us who love you are your cover."

A few remarks about cover: One summer, I spent a weekend in the country with married people—my friend Squirrel from Palo Alto and her husband; he never liked me. Ten years earlier, he'd thrown out some papers Squirrel had been keeping in their attic for me, including a poster-size framed photograph of me in a nineteen-sixties advertisement for Jonathan Logan, which the photographer had made just for me. It was as if this man were throwing me away. He did things like that, and my friend defended him, incessantly. ("He's just a little boy," she said when he threw a crumpled-up paper napkin in my face at the lunch table once. I myself would rather be dead than be married to a man like him.) When I walked into the kitchen early on the Sunday morning, he was alone with their eighteen-month-old granddaughter—a baby who a few months before had kissed me sweetly on the lips and called me "Atson." He looked up at me and, right in the baby's ear, he said, in a condescending, whispery voice, "Alison's *crazy,* she's *crazy.*"

Later that day, their son, with his wife—Puppy Jane and I were in the back seat with the baby—drove me, under orders, frantically late, to the train station. When we had missed the train, we ended up chasing it from town to town, the baby screaming all the while. It was raining hard, and I had this flimsy carrying case with holes in it for Puppy Jane, but nevertheless the young man and his wife drove off with their baby and left me and Puppy Jane in the hard rain under a rickety umbrella at a train station without an overpass, because they had a dinner date with her parents, whom they saw often. If I had been a married woman, or Puppy Jane had been a real baby, they would never have done that.

The truth is, it can be a form of actual day-to-day social torture to pretend not to notice the little dishes of poison that married people offer you all the time. And especially people who have children. They convey that there isn't any point to existence if you haven't got married and had a baby. I've noticed that insufferable wives expect me to think it's the saddest thing possible to be childless. And although it's truly nobody's business what I think about childlessness, when they ask me about it, I lie—absolutely lie—anyway. I say, "Well, it's something I just don't think about." It's unpremeditated lying.

And in fact I never wanted a baby. I never did think about it, except for that pronoun Dr. Cederquist presented me with. I never had baby dolls when I was little; they looked fat and naked and dead. The *Little Women* dolls my mother bought for me one Christmas had creamy skin and thin bodies and those paisley-print dresses, which fit them so nicely around the bodice, and the expressions on their faces weren't stupid.

At a party not long ago, a depressed man I know—it is his depression I love him for—took all his boy baby's clothes off just to show me what a strong body the baby had. He was tall for a baby and had big shoulders and what looked like actual muscles in his thighs. This depressed man later told me over the telephone that the only thing in life that made him feel good was playing with the baby in the mornings. He said he was certain the baby liked him. At that moment—just for a few horrible seconds—I felt plain jealousy, instead of fury. I was happy for him, but it was clear that I was fatally left out.

Anyway, the whole point is that mothers have *made their own friends*. Literally, they made them out of their bodies. No justifiable *tristesse* of mine, or, for that matter, exultation—about a man, or a Nobel Prize in Physics I'd just won—would make any difference to one of these mothers, next to those living things she had made for herself.

It's exhausting to be in the company of married people, with children or no; it forces me into a state of emergency alert, in which I have to rescue myself from interrogation and public disgrace. (Beguiling, on-cue self-reserve is tiring.) Their incomprehension and condescending fakeness are thick in the air, no matter how they try to hide it. ("No, no, it's our treat," a twenty-dollar bill shoved back and forth across the table.) The fun part for me—like the thrill successful bank robbers must feel—is, after an escape from the restaurant, gloriously alone, to flag down a taxi, whiz across the Park, slam the taxi door on Sixty-eighth Street, and then run half a block and up the stairs to my pretty room, where the animals, with their unabashed enthusiasm, are waiting.

There was a night, however, when Mr. Normalcy's wife and children were away that he cooked dinner for me at his apartment, in between rounds of sex. Watching him cook—he was leaning over the stove and I was sitting at the kitchen table—I felt what it was like to be a person a guy like this had dinner at home with. It was paradise. He was like a whole human family in one person. I stayed the night, and he made breakfast for me, too. "I'm jealous that you get to wake up with yourself in the morning," he said. I loved him for saying that. When I left, out on the street with myself again, I had not even a frisson of regret, though I was swaying a little from the abrupt orphandom.

Once or twice over the years, he said, "You don't like me that much," which was both true and a lie. When I see him now, years later, at a party, I still wish he would take care of me—not divorce his wife and marry me but bring me a Diet Coke with lemon and be my brother.

. . .

Out in the world, all kinds of people thought that what Personality Plus said was heartening and important; around School, he hummed to himself in the corridors like a warning that he was radioactive. He did things for me all the time—things I wished a man would do, like call all the way from Singapore when I was sick. He once offered me the use of his apartment for a dinner party I was giving. He put a framed photograph of Toast on the desk in his office where family photos would normally be.

One day, he gave me three office-supply-store stamps with an ink pad. He walked in and silently lined them up on my desk. They said "Confirmation," "Approved," and "Do Not Bend." When he would come up to my desk in the cubicle and stand there in front of me, humming and impressive, I felt thankfulness and hope, which might have been what other people call love. He was the only one who made me feel that particular way.

"I think you are the most romantic writer on the eighteenth floor, Episcopalian skirt and all," he said once as he lumbered past the cubicle.

One night after I'd worked at School for a couple of years, I went with him to a bar that served tropical drinks, kind of a fake Tahitian bar. They had Christmas decorations at one end of the bar—Jesus and animals and a manger, a small tree with colored bulbs—and a string of blinking white lights above all the bottles of liquor. His big hands were on the wooden counter—they were very big hands—and he kept twirling a deep-blue plastic gardenia that was floating in his vermouth cassis around and around. Neither of us knew what to say, because we were outside School, and because he never said much anyway.

Eventually I noticed his wrist hair showing above the cuff of his pale-pink shirt. "You're a little like King Kong," I said. "The rest of me isn't," he said.

He was attentive to me—he took me out for a ride around New York Harbor, and wrote me a note: "I will be reading avidly, of course, everything you write"—so attentive that George said, in his emphatic way, "You *belong* to him." I didn't. But Personality Plus always took my side when there was the slightest disapproval of me; he was incredibly loyal. Once, when he and Mr. Normalcy and I had lunch, and Mr. Normalcy said something indirectly insulting to me, he subtly annihilated him; he diminished him in a way I've never heard a man diminish another man. I don't even remember the words, I was too bowled over by their effect on me. It was simply thrilling.

For a while, he was as if beside himself with affection—I have postcards and handwritten notes in a neat pile in the back of my good-sweater drawer to prove it to myself. The first time he came over to my room, we worried about it, his adultery. We had talked about the worry on the telephone a few days before. I kind of knew going to bed with him would wreck the Do Not Bend confirmation, but I didn't say no.

I was ready hours early. The animals and I waited for him, didn't know exactly what to do with the time, so the three of us just sat there on the bed and listened to the radio:

"July 14, 1937," I wrote down. " 'The Old Stompin' Ground.' Willie the Lion Smith and his cubs, Frankie Newton on trumpet . . . Fats Waller doing 'T'aint Nobody's Business if I Do.' The next radio station had Rush Limbaugh, so I turned to Supertramp."

Then there he was. I was wearing a blue Chinese silk bathrobe and under it a long white cotton nightgown, like one a young girl might wear, plain but like a dress, with spaghetti straps. When he walked in—bright-blue pullover, jeans; a God-fearing Yankee—I knew he felt excessively nervous, not just because he'd come over but because he was fundamentally distrustful "in a more global way," as Europe might have put it.

He had the prettiest legs, wholesome legs, but no one would have guessed, because he wasn't a showoff about the way he looked. However, he had very wishy legs—with muscles showing in them, though I don't think he customarily did anything purposefully athletic. I liked his calves and I liked just being with his legs, knowing they were there. And in comparison with my five feet five he seemed so tall that he obliterated my existence, and for this I was grateful.

He lay across the top of my bed and told me about his growing up. Though I had known him at School for a long time, I hadn't known anything about his history. It was a very good story—set in a land of no people. I had my hand on his face while he told it, because I liked his face; his eyes were like Toast's. The street lamp shining through the colored glass of the windows—an entirely different thing at night—gave the story itself a worrisome light. He said he didn't remember people when he thought back. What he remembered was Guy Lombardo and his Royal Canadians singing, "Enjoy yourself, enjoy yourself, it's later than you think."

He developed quite an attachment to the plain white nightgown over time, mentioned it in a graceful way in letters he sent when he was out of town. Later on, he sometimes gathered Puppy Jane's toys onto the bed—a brown rabbit all chewed at; a red knit ball made to look like a strawberry, of a size to fit in her mouth; a small bear with no arms (she'd removed them); a plastic bone—to make a little puppet show for her. The brown rabbit was the main character. Puppy swallowed over and over with the excitement of it.

One time, after we had been in my bed for a while, he got up and sat on the windowsill and said, "Guilt." Then he got dressed and went off to take his grown children out to dinner. Most of the time, it didn't matter that much if anyone thought of me as a "bad girl." I didn't think it—it didn't cross my mind. But now, when this man I did kind of literally cherish was abruptly—intentionally—gone, I had an unexpected reaction: I wanted to give up, repent, move to Mississippi and work in a bakery.

.   .   .

One thing I have to say is that, in addition to not being blond in any sense of the word, I'm not that pretty. But I swear—on Puppy Jane and Toast—that a lot of people thought I was. I could feel the men at School and elsewhere react to what they called my prettiness. Monique said one time, in a coffee shop on Madison, "It's the *regard,* Aleece, it's the *regard.*" Whatever it was, a lot of men wanted to get up closer to it, and they did.

The first day I went to School—the day I walked down there and had poached eggs—Europe followed me downstairs in the elevator and around the lobby at the end of the School day. That didn't have to do with rational thinking. He wasn't shy about the flirtation and he wasn't ambivalent about it, either. He had had a prettier life in prettier places than the other men at School, and he paid me real romantic attention. One day, when all my favorites were around the cubicle at once, he hung from the doorway molding with both hands, as if on a jungle gym. At another moment he said he thought life was "endless," and I wrote to him every day to ease his boredom:

Yesterday George said I have to write a page for him by dinner-time on Thursday night. He said I COULDN'T BE THE

SMARTEST PERSON WHO DOESN'T DO ANYTHING
FOREVER. But the truth is I'm distracted by the image of
your hair when you came in this morning. Something tousled
about it. Was it the wind? Your hair is usually all in one place.
Or did you have a mad thought in the elevator and ruffle it up
all by yourself?

Many women liked Europe—and why not?—and he liked
them, too, but I was the only one at School. I knew there were a
lot of women, because it was my job to answer the phone, and
they called. Later, when I had my own office, we would kiss
while leaning against the locked door.

Sometimes I would take the day off, a "sick day," to race all
around town all morning finding garter belts and things, pray-
ing that I didn't run into anyone from work. He would be coming over later on those days.

The first time he came to my room, around Christmas, he
opened the big closet doors and then closed them, as if to see if
anyone was in there. Because there was never a sofa in my room,
he would sit with me on the refectory table, beside the typewriter. On the side near the windows, with the table as a sofa,
we would embrace each other in a proper kind of affectionate
way, like normal teen-agers in the fifties in someone's parents'
living room.

He called my room Toast-sur-Mer, and we had all-day sex—
and I mean all day long without a break—but then he would
talk about his children. That made me want to die, but,
instead, I pathetically put strawberries on one of my mother's
plates and set it on the long table, and he sat there and ate
them. Then he left. With him, I kind of looked forward to the
next day at School, because there was a niceness in his sheepish-
ness. After he had left my apartment, though, I'd go out and

buy, say, a scarf that cost hundreds of dollars which later I didn't even like.

He had shirts that when they were on him in my room took borderline *tristesse* right out of my head; a pale-pale-green one, and two I called *pêche*—one a lighter shade, or more washed than the other. And he had blue shirts, of course. In white shirts he looked particularly pristine in a perverse way: a thicker cotton weave, and flimsy cotton, too. Fitzgerald was a brilliant man, to know about Daisy and those shirts. I liked Europe to keep one of these shirts on for as long as he could stand it, those afternoons, so that the next time I saw him in it, at School, I would know exactly what it felt like close up, my hands on it and under it, creases in the schoolboy starch, a dampness.

We'd sit on the table or else on the windowsill, kissing, and then we would lie on the bed in our clothes—*in all our clothes,* so as to re-create that "I can't live without you or it" feeling—for an inordinate amount of time. Then, there was this other version of sex that would happen—ever so slightly *normale:* take off the clothes, both of you, and when you can feel the other one's skin, and everything about the other person, you definitively aren't by yourself anymore. You're taking this BIG CHANCE on the up-closeness. What if he figures out, once and forever, what's the matter with you? And if you've waited a really long time, as we did those times, it's just this ecstasy that has nothing to do with anything else. *That's* sex, no little depressive trimmings whatsoever but just pleasure. There aren't any "Do you like me?" *pensées,* either.

In a short story, Harold wrote (not about me), "She's been in love with all of us, one by one." I have no idea what *love,* in that sentence, meant or means, but that's the way I felt, except with a fair amount of simultaneousness. At School, Europe seemed,

sometimes, to have a harsh spirit, and often made mean, cutting remarks about people (declared that their emotions were
"misplaced," say, whereas they may not have been). But when
he came to my room on Sixty-eighth Street he was very romantic, almost Romantic, Keats at age ten. The look on his face
when he was going to kiss me was almost too sad, so that I'd
have to look away.

And he was romantic with his arms: no heaviness of heart
lessened the way he used his arms in an embrace, wound around
me wholeheartedly, just a stand-up-in-the-middle-of-the-
room-wearing-clothes embrace, as though he might have been
wishing I was even his mother—for a minute. "Affection and
sex are scarce," he said once. "When I see you the distance
between now and true nothingness is shorter," I wrote to him
later, sadly. But in odd circumstances like ours there was no real
place to put the romantic impulse. I don't know if romance
looks happy, his didn't, and that made it closer to what I imagine love is.

Bulletin:

Dear A.:
I waited here for many moons—well, many moments—but you
were (and stayed) elsewhere . . .

One time, he was going away on a long vacation, and he
came to see me in my office, closed the door and locked it, and
kissed me goodbye very nicely. He seemed sorry to be saying
goodbye. I should have felt all right, but I didn't. I followed
him in the elevator down to the lobby, where he refused—he
was a stubborn man, anyway—to turn around and talk to me.

That evening, I walked to the pet store on Lexington near my
apartment, and when I looked into the cages I nearly fainted: I

wanted a silky white dog—something totally mine—but did I actually want to live with some little animal? I put a white dog, a girl dog, on "hold." The woman there asked me if I wanted bows in her hair. The next morning, when I brought the dog home in a cardboard box and she followed me to the refrigerator, I wasn't sure if I liked her or not. That was Puppy Jane.

One year I had a dress that all the men liked a lot. The first time George saw it, he said, "This is our Dust Bowl dress," and there was something already-old about it, as if it had been mine for years, even though I'd gone to the small store on Madison that week and, after trying it on fast, bought it new: but it looked as if it had already been worn thin by hot sun in summer and men putting their hands all over it.

This dress wasn't any big deal of a dress; it was just light cotton, a smallish print, faded orange and yellow. Besides its Dust Bowl appeal, it had numerous buttons down to a dropped waistline below the hips, short sleeves cut close, and a cut-out neck, and, best of all, the fabric stayed close to the body but was loose at the same time. The print looked blurred, not a stupid, finite print. Everyone at School liked this dress: "I love that dress." "Nice dress." Even Monique, when I met her on First Avenue for a tuna sandwich one day in it, said, as soon as she saw me on the sidewalk, "*Aleece!* What a pretty *dress!*" (Usually she didn't say what I wore was pretty unless she had decided I should wear it, and I'd bought this un-French dress all by myself.) At School, Veronica Geng asked me a few times with some urgency if she could borrow it and make a pattern from it.

But the person who really admired the dress better than anybody else was Europe. He seemed to understand the dress, and when he unbuttoned all the buttons as they went down, I forgot about "being" altogether. He referred to it as "the orange dress," though it wasn't really an orange dress at all, but he liked having a term for it.

He would come over to my room at the start of summer, before going away, and I would wear it for him. Before he pushed the buzzer and I let him in, I'd sit in the green wicker chair and think about him, as if I were wishing for him: for putting my arms around the somewhat stiff shirt he'd be wearing, stiff from professional ironing and the perfect amount of starch. It was actual, painful longing right in my chest, and then, when he showed up at the front door on Sixty-eighth Street, I'd say to myself, "How about that?"

The sitting-in-the-chair wishing never lasted long; for one thing, Europe was very punctual, so I'd look at my watch and wish for, say, only five minutes before the buzzer would ring, at around noon (it would have been a School day), and then I'd get up, go and push the button on the panel beside my door, and wait there, sometimes fiddling with the top of my stocking and the garter to make sure it was attached securely. I'd hear the outer and inner doors close, footsteps on the staircase. Then he'd knock a little, not much, and I'd open the door. Even though I'd seen him the day before at School, I'd be in a state of inexplicable surprise that he was right there, even though he was right there in the doorway in this same way for six years.

What he would say was "Oh, the orange dress!"—like that, as if he hadn't seen it for decades, as if it weren't an old friend, reliable, which it was, but instead were brand-new to him, also an inexplicable surprise, maybe to counter his innate boredom and discomfort with, as far as I could tell, nearly everything except sex. One time, in preparation for his arrival, I had, the night before, actually hand-washed the little clothes on two

bears I have on the windowsill. (I've had them since I was five
or so.) He commented on the cleanness of the small white knit
pullover and the extremely small not-pink-anymore polka-dot
dress. "So clean," he said, which was unlike him. Was more like
me. Then he put his hands under the orange dress, lifted it up
a little, then more. I would have shaved my legs very carefully,
so that they were smooth under the silky stockings he'd
requested, and put on some slippery hand lotion he liked.
Whatever he wanted me to do, I did it.

I would always have new underwear, which was easy to
choose in a store, because he would have written notes about
what kind he felt like spending the afternoon with; sometimes
cotton in nice weather, or silk, not lacy. He was my lover. I
know that I put these notes into a gray envelope and into a very
messy closet in the hallway, with all kinds of books and papers
squashed in there going every which way, on many shelves, but
I can't find the gray envelope when I look for it now, because
notebooks and paperbacks fall on my head from the top shelf
and I give up quickly. It's dangerous to open the door. (George
opened it the first time he came over, and said, "Just think, the
whole place could look like this.") I do want to find it, though, so
I can bury it somewhere, the way some people bury their cat's
ashes in Central Park. Europe often said I should take myself,
on one of my breaks from School, on a vacation to Portugal, so
perhaps I could bury his notes in Portugal. One of them (I'd
copied part of what he'd written onto a shopping list) was a
suggestion that I wear a white dress, "modified schoolgirl, skirt
with a swing"—an "accessibility," he called it. When I was on
jury duty one October, I called him at School from the vile
bank of phone booths by the jury room, where people used to
line up to call to complain about the judges and the waiting,

and he said, "Think of yourself as a romantic person among strangers."

I like to think about sitting with him on the refectory table back then, that orange dress raised a little higher, higher still, kissing, nothing to lean against except him, shoes dangling. I would look quickly around the room and be so pleased, so proud at how I'd cleaned it all up for him. There's an old note that I just found, copied over, that I'd given to him in late spring, May, before he came over to my room:

> Last night when I was scrubbing with Fantastik and Lysol foam, I sat down for a rest and listened to Fats Waller on the jazz station do a 1937 number called "Spring Cleaning." Mr. Waller (himself, I think) sang, "Spring cleaning—getting ready for love—that's the real cleaning."

I once wrote him a half-dozen stories about all the women whom he'd ever mentioned in a particular way, or who had called him too many times at School, or whom I imagined he could like. I had one of them—call her Charlotte Rampling— wearing the famous "orange dress," although by an idiotic, really lush poolside in Brentwood, California, where I wouldn't be too jealous. I could be generous with my dress with him in this way. In these stories—I would laugh and laugh and laugh as I wrote them—his wife never got to wear the "orange dress."

Once at School I'd asked him, "Are you my friend?," and he'd answered, "Oh God, yes. Are you doubting that? Did I do something?"

"No," I said, "I just feel crazy."

And he said, "Well, you can eliminate that."

I wrote down things he said at one time or another as he said them, but, whatever I said or didn't say to him in response, no written thing was as wishy as being with him in my room. I never told Harold about Europe's coming over to my room, but he did know something, or see the effect of it. After I'd just spent a day at Toast-sur-Mer, Harold, in my cubicle, said, "You look ravishing. You're happier when you're bossy. More alive."

Sometimes when Europe left my room (I'd hear the down-stairs door shut and I'd try to see him from the window, but he was always too close to the buildings), I wanted to obliterate the entire concept of Toast-sur-Mer: to crush it to smithereens and stamp on it and have the life go out of it in the same way I used to stamp out cigarettes on the sidewalk—back and forth with a fairly wide high heel. I wanted the nice little thoughts of him knocked right out of my head, to make sure the time I'd just spent with him was extremely dead. I couldn't actually have him, and that was that.

After about ten minutes, I would allow the nice thoughts back in, would give them permission, which was a really special present to myself—just missing him, a normal heartsickness. But then I might think of him out there somewhere—worse, at home—and things would get bad again. Really bad. The dizzi-ness that snuffs out fun-in-a-way heartsickness and replaces it with plain emptiness is like an attack of gray ice all over the place. And no sounds. Putting the side of my face on Puppy Jane's pink, fragile stomach—straining not to lean too hard— helped at times, but it didn't break down the ice completely.

.   .   .

How the emptiness itself goes away and things become man-ageable again is unclear but oddly dependable. It's amazing the way a jubilation can take its place, with a little Coltrane, or some rice pudding. Maybe it's true that I'm happier with animals or a French dress or palm trees than with human company. A postcard George sent me some years ago has a picture of five palm trees in a row under a blue sky (I've seen them look just like that from the terrace of the hotel in Beverly Hills) and, on the back, in the middle of the card, in ballpoint pen, "Get the point?"

My whole life I've thought about people—and thought and thought about them—but they've never been right there in front of me, even when they've been in front of me, because I'm just me alone thinking, trying not to get sent to Agnew. But sometimes, when Europe was with me in my room, I felt an entirely different way. It seemed to me that he brought the highest reverence—tactile worship, even—to being up close to another person. He directed his entire consciousness toward me. I felt that presence physically, no matter where he was. But in my room it was his gift to make all of himself present to me, and I wasn't just me, by myself, hacking my way through the wilderness.

Five Thanksgivings ago, Billy the Fish listened to me make roast chicken over the phone—we talked for hours. Actually, I've stayed friends with most of my old boyfriends, which matters to me. When I'm absolutely alone, though, I can think it's somewhat fun to feel sorry for myself; it's a kind of soothing attention; it isn't coming from anyone else. If I didn't have some self-pity, I might have a severe temptation to push smug Mrs. So-and-So down a couple of flights of stairs, or go down them myself. Self-pity makes me not think of that. Also, self-pity can make me do things: wash my hair or clean the apartment, drag twelve pounds of laundry up Madison to the

Chinese place. Then I can make babyish food for myself and wrap myself up in a bandage of fresh sheets. Or write a letter. Or call Francine. In a way, I don't see why my pleasure with self-pity should give anyone else a bad opinion of me or why I should care if it does. I don't know what the Bible says about it, except that—without being an official commandment—it's a thing not to do; but then, that makes self-pity like an outlaw by my side, a naughtily illegal friend doing me some good.

The opposite way to look at it is this: self-pity, when it's like a disease, is a refusal to get the point about—to really see—the other person. If I am dizzy and sad about Europe, say, who is walking down the stairs to Sixty-eighth Street (silent, *cher* loafers on the decaying brown plaid carpet), then I have already refused to consider how that man was a non-English-speaking boy on another continent more than fifty years ago. And, as I can see whenever I do go beyond the self-pity disease, part of the outcome of what had seemed his glorious life is that, after a lot of sex, he's also alone, walking fast one flight down on the cheap carpet.

"YIELD TO IT. LET IT
WASH OVER YOU"

At School, George comes by with his heavy footsteps. He begins his sentence before he sees me, and I hear it: *"Darling,"* he says, still out of sight, "I just want you to know that every moment is torture until dinner." Starting when I'd been at School a year or so—once a week for seven months at a stretch, then skipping a month, maybe, then starting again—Harold organized these dinners: with his wife, Ellen, George, me, the novelist Howard Coale, sometimes four or five others. We would go to an Afghan restaurant on Ninth Avenue, to Un Deux Trois on West Forty-fourth Street, to the Boulevard, up on Broadway near the Brodkeys', once to a dingy place in upper Times Square called Tin Pan Alley, and to two Italian restaurants in the West Forties, one called Mamma's.

For me, perhaps the most thrilling part was leaving School property with Harold and George. George would take my arm on the street, as if we were going to dance at a cotillion, and walking between the two of them I felt I had fortresses on either side of me. Because I wanted to be with both of them, and to be like them, to *be* them, in a way—wished for it, at any rate—and because of their all-pervasive energy all over the corridors at School, well, they *were* fortresses.

George walked fast; even a stroll was fast with him. The walks to the dinners, like the dinners, were full of energy and impatience.

Howard Coale had been a student of Harold's at Cornell and was still young, twenty-eight, with brown hair cut straight and shortish; brown eyes set far apart; an unprominent nose that looked different when you looked straight at him than it did in profile; small, perfect ears; a voluptuous mouth that made him seem eager, though I was never exactly sure what he was eager about.

The Afghan restaurant was a tiny place, with short white tablecloths, in the Fifties somewhere, and they served skimpy pieces of lamb-on-a-stick, some dusty-looking kind of dark rice, the flat bread that tastes like absolutely nothing. Howard says now that at the dinners he was "crippled with nervousness, sometimes," but it didn't show: he would lean back in his chair and rock it, never fall off.

At dinner, Howard's eyes could look confused and hurt but at the next moment close to ecstatic. When he'd glance my way or say something in response to what I'd just said, he would look or speak as if he were certain he'd understood exactly what I'd meant, though often I thought he hadn't. The dinners were crazy, too. Howard could get furious that any of us considered craziness charming or adorable. He went too far with that theory, I thought, and could be unpleasant about it. As George said to him, one of those nights, "*How-ard,* you're right about things. . . . But you're also just a little bit *wrong.*"

Nevertheless, at the dinners Howard would be quick to turn an incipiently depressing thing I'd been saying into something high-spirited. Harold might have asked me some unanswerable question about what I thought about my mother, and I'd answer with a story about wanting to kill Mother in Atherton. "Near San Francisco," I'd say—to explain where she lived to a newcomer—and Howard would interrupt, as if meaning to correct me, "*San Fiasco*." So on the whole having Howard there was a shaft of light in what was potentially a dark chamber— beyond food and crazy charm, a potential combat zone between Harold and George. "I only see people like you as characters," George said to Harold one Thursday night. "You don't see people as real people, and that's why you don't have any characters," Harold said back. Howard failed us that one time. He said nothing.

Once, Harold's haircutter came to a dinner, with his wife, and also with the person who later wrote Harold's obit in the *Times*. "I cut Harold's hair," the haircutter said, as if he were talking about tailoring suits for the Czar. Harold, in his dark clothes and silver-brown hair, was the elder reigning authority. At these dinners especially, he was a proud man. Mostly Ellen agreed with Harold's world view as expressed, but other times she'd say, "Oh, *Har*old," and Howard and I would be relieved.

Harold would speak to Dante Alighieri about you and put you in Paradise, was the understanding in the air over the table—just let him get to a phone. But the point of the dinners, I thought, was to talk about whatever came into our heads. "The three of us talking about our minds," George said anticipatorily one afternoon at School before a dinner. It could be outlandish non sequiturs. You could really say something that wasn't understood by anyone there and not get into trouble. (On the other hand, however, sometimes if you disagreed with a statement—Shakespeare's position in the universe, say—you might get shut out.) I could talk about Toast, and did. "She's furrier than fur," I'd say. And no one asked me what that meant. And the dinners were operatic: Harold would talk in his Harvard Bible mode about my background (which to him had an allure about it that eluded me), and then he'd go on about who I was, according to him. "Alison is the princess of the twentieth century," and George would say, "No. Alison is more the *duchess* of the twentieth century." And George would add, in defense of his last statement, "Harold, what you don't *know* is . . ." What Harold actually said at these times didn't matter too much to me: it was the tone (never lying). He'd lay down the law about me. Then he might say, "Howard is a Jewish Quaker from Philadelphia who's like Stephen Dedalus."

I was mostly quiet at the dinners. George, sitting next to me, sprawling, would put his hands under his broadcloth shirt and yank on it somehow, and it was one of the few times in my life when I felt I had a real partner. One Thursday night, George remarked, apropos of a dress that I had on: "Not defined by a partner, so Search for Self through Bias and Cut." Whenever I'd say nothing, he'd stand in for me, one hand on his Tanqueray gin, the other ruffling his hair, looking to me a lot, as if I were a person he knew intimately and he were my interpreter.

At Mamma's on Ninth Avenue one night, George began yelling about Little Richard and why Little Richard was *Important* in AMERICA. Harold and his wife were hoping not to be with George in public after that—too boisterous for them— but I thought he'd never been funnier or more right.

Harold called me not long afterward and said he wanted me to invite someone else out to dinner—another man, not George, someone I would come up with—and that way he and Ellen and me and this mystery guest could be friends.

"But, Harold, I don't have an appropriate suitor, you know that," I said.

"Not a suitor. No one likes you all *that* much."

"Maybe that's true," I said.

He tried to be comforting: "But nobody likes anybody all that much, it's just moments—you know that." And, after a pause, he added, "*I'm* the one who likes you all that much, but if you get to know me better your life will be considerably shorter. Hang up now or I'll start to cry."

Our very last night at Un Deux Trois—one of the noisiest places in New York, but it had been a favorite—there were more than the usual five or six at our table: a waitress started calling it "the dangerous table." Harold's wife was there, and some younger male writers George and I didn't know, who all adored Harold; Howard was there, and Veronica Geng, who had been George's editor at School for a time, and who, with longtime affectionate respect as well as brilliance, was a champion at standing up to both George and Harold. Harold had been talking about what we might think if we bothered to think harder; he analyzed what every one of us had been thinking up till now and what would happen to us in the future. (He was eerily right about things.) Then, in the drunken argument that put an end to our evenings together, George and Harold began fighting about the unfairness of God in the Old Testament. George had an extremely loud screaming fit. Since I couldn't have cared less about the subject, I didn't have a point of view, and don't recall who took which side; I certainly didn't take a side. Both of them wanted fond confirmation, and I gave it wholeheartedly to both of them every five minutes or so. It didn't help. Harold said to George, as if looking for a truce of sorts, "I introduced you to Patsy Cline, Dante, and Alison Rose." And then to me, "The two most depressed human beings in the world—on your string."

"No more putting together the Dream Team," George said as we left.

After the Big Fight about God, George didn't come to the dinners anymore. "Not having George at dinner is like taking the oxygen atom out of a water molecule," Howard said, and more people I didn't know showed up and the dinners became more social and public. One week Harold asked me to call and invite twenty people, and most of them showed up.

"A lack of bad feelings would be divine," George said after the dinners were over for him. And, "The importance of Harold Brodkey will be said and done within a reasonable amount of time." He paused. "We're like Austria and Hungary. It's a mistake to be linked right now."

There had been a night, earlier on, when George and I went to a reading Harold was doing with a younger writer, downtown in the East Village, in a very small space, little tables close together. George spread himself out at our tiny table, and as Harold and the young man were reading talked at the top of his lungs and laughed out loud, and if there'd been a pistol on the table he would have murdered everyone in the room. Among other remarks, he said, "None of these people have any experience or *information*." (George often said that people had no "information" because they refused to have it.) I felt that night that what he was perceiving and expressing was something real—something atrocious coming soon, here on earth.

"He was commedia dell'arte as Dracula," Howard, who was there, said of George that night, however. (But I still do think George wasn't wrong.) And later Harold told me that what George and I had done "against" him was "suicidal."

One time, in a dark bar where businessmen went, George said, after he had taken me to lunch and a dinosaur movie, "*Some* came a hundred miles and spent a hundred dollars just to take you to the *movies*." He said it loud. He said everything so loud and decidedly it was as if nothing could ever frighten me again. He would stand in the cubicle doorway while I took messages on the phone. Once, he crossed his arms as he watched me ignore the phone ringing and said, "Answer the phone. I'll still be here." Another time, he said, "Darling, we're *almost* like other people," and even Dr. Cederquist, whom I'd then been seeing for thirty years, wrote it down.

Later that same night, over a drink, George said, speaking in general, "You get to keep what you have, but you don't get *any more*," and added, speaking in particular, "Since we didn't have very much, we had to Keep On Going." Another time he made a remark about "having spent all one's life in prison for some very good reason." Not long afterward: "If only I could take the sunlight at face value."

I said to George, "Without your George-ness, I don't know."

As he was passing my doorway one day around this time, George said—in fact, he came up close to me and whispered it in my ear—"Everything is perfect now, and scary." He meant we were close now in a way that was scary to him.

"What a lucky break," Mr. Normalcy said one day.

"Why do you say that?" I asked him.

"Because George is lucky to have you obsessed with him. I mean, he could have gone through life without that."

I had a series of good dreams about George. One of them was just George and me in my apartment on Doheny in Los Angeles. He was helping me throw away all these things I hadn't thought of in twenty years—shelves and shelves of things. He threw away some platform shoes I'd bought on Camden Drive in Beverly Hills and also a really cheap quilt that an old rich friend had given me. We were wrapping them up in white blankets and getting rid of them by throwing them over the balcony onto the sunbathers and into the swimming pool. We were listening to Elvis and the Temptations while we did this.

. . .

When I first knew George, he was living in the city, on Tenth Avenue at Forty-sixth Street, in Hell's Kitchen, though he already had his house in the country. I went over to his apartment with Harold and Howard, after a dinner, and he had an axe-like thing hung on one wall and also a note I had written to him. The apartment was otherwise just about empty. There was a man who lived downstairs, and one evening George and this man had a real, physical fight (I don't know about what) in the man's apartment, just before George was to come over to my house for dinner. He came over anyway, and when I saw him in my doorway he had kind of a black eye, or more; he looked like a man who had been beaten up. He lay on top of my bed to rest and recover. There isn't anywhere else in my room to do that comfortably. I put the pink-and-blue blanket I had knit twenty years before on top of him. Then Howard arrived and pulled one of the chairs from the refectory table over to the bed and read Wallace Stevens to George. It was an odd surprise having George there, and Howard was a good reader, with a voice like an American Jeremy Irons, and I could hear him from the kitchen as I turned the chicken over, basted it, made a salad, Monique's vinaigrette. Later on, after Howard left, George said to me, "May I sleep here? In a discreet way?" It wasn't like overnights with Squirrel or Dill; no twin beds.

In the morning, I had to go to School, so I left him in my pink room with Toast, his face all swollen and distorted. There had been a snowstorm up where he lived in the country, so he couldn't get back there, and because of the fight he couldn't go back to his apartment. I couldn't wait to go home at the end of the day and see him in my room. He didn't seem unhappy to see me.

George invited me up to his house in the country for Christmas. We arranged to meet by the clock at Grand Central on Christmas Eve to take the train north. I remember him standing by the information booth in an old Brooks Brothers coat. There was a sturdiness about his body and an uncontrived, East Coast straggliness to his thinnish blond hair. It was easy to pretend he was my boyfriend, though he never really was. I knew that, but I had knitted him a scarf, and he was wearing it. On the train, he read me things from the *Times,* and we laughed. He had a twinklingness in his blue eyes. In his big living room he had just a few bare twigs stuck in a utilitarian pail for Christmas decorations. He took me to see friends of his, and to church, and we sang with the congregation. On Christmas Day, he gave me a bracelet that had belonged to his grandmother, just the way a normal man might do with a normal woman.

It was the next June that Harold noticed that women were wearing miniskirts again, and decided to write a Talk of the Town piece about it. Perhaps because he had once said of me, "Look how affectionately she's holding the phone," he asked me to call up some people—the Russian poet Joseph Brodsky, family-values Senator Jesse Helms, and my mother among them—and ask each of them about the miniskirt. Brodsky had recently won the Nobel Prize; he'd also once done five years of hard labor near the White Sea. I felt fairly idiotic asking him about the miniskirt, but at the end of the conversation ("Would you wear one if you were a girl?" "If I were a girl, I would go for it. It creates a mild tension, a suspense"), Brodsky said I could call him whenever I wanted and ask him anything.

MOTHER: The miniskirt? Oh, that's about ethics and ego and self-images. It's distressing and disturbing on women whose legs aren't good. Fashion is unkind. Women like to be appreciated. As do men and dogs.

ALISON: Do you think your friends will shorten their skirts?

MOTHER: Maybe the uninteresting people will.

ALISON: Why do you know uninteresting people?

MOTHER: You can't always have interesting people in your life. You have to have some flops around the edges.

Harold put his part of the piece and my part of the piece together and took it upstairs. This became "Brodkey/Rose," as it was called on the publishing schedule. There was nothing like seeing my name printed out with his like that. What I'd written wasn't much different from the letters I gave him at School. The questions I'd asked were the way I talked. Harold hadn't changed any of that. "Tell Harold he's saintly," Penelope said, and added, "an adjective I wouldn't use across the board."

Veronica Geng, who was good-looking, and, what's more, wore miniskirts, had a high regard for the piece, and she said that one of the letters I'd written to her had "a beginning, a middle, and an end," and that I could make it into a short story. She also suggested I write a piece about a new autobiography by a famous actress. "Don't read it, just make it up," she said. But I was too nervous to do either of those things.

What with my preoccupations and halfhearted phone-answering practices, I was more or less fired from my cubicle at School, not that long afterward, though none of the authorities used the word. Ten or twelve of the writers, all men, went upstairs to intercede; it was like men going off to war in uniform to fight for me. Harold and Personality Plus took me out to a French lunch off Tenth Avenue on my last official day. They were tall on either side of me as we walked over from School. Things seemed normal in a way, though; nothing was especially sad, and nothing that mattered was over with. The odd thing was I didn't write down anything they said that day, because I wanted the feeling of that particular, actual life. The whole situation was awful, but I was rescued.

Chip McGrath, who was now Robert Gottlieb's deputy editor, had been having an ongoing conversation with George, trying to get him to write Talk stories again (he'd written them for years in the sixties and seventies, was a real magician at it, but hadn't written unsigned pieces for some time). George must have said something about not wanting to come down to the city to do reporting anymore, and McGrath said (George told me), "What about Alison Rose?"

George called me at about eight o'clock in the morning to announce with accelerated George enthusiasm, in an all-points-bulletin voice, that we were going to write Talk stories together. "Darling, would you like that?" he asked. His voice was boyish-shy, but just for a moment. I didn't say anything, just kept still on the bed. Someone had once said Talk stories were as much a strict literary form as sonnets.

George said we'd be partners, a team, that I could use his office at School, that it would be my office—our office. George is the only man who said "we" and "our" when he talked to me. He would say "our life." Chip McGrath called, too. About George's mind, he said to me, "Yield to it. Let it wash over you."

George came and gave me lessons on how to think about interviewing a subject for a Talk story: "Look for poignancy in the noble thing, the optimistic thing," he said, and I was writing it down in a big royal-blue spiral notebook. Toast sat watching. "Glimpse genuine joy, in a way, in the middle of world horror," George said, in the context of a Talk subject, a devoted dog groomer, whom I'd be interviewing soon. And on another subject, a man who was expert at twirling a rodeo rope and would be coming through town: "Be a servant of his energy, a stimulant. Allow him to take delight in his own life. His life is your life. Find common sense and sweetness."

The ideas for the stories came from George; I never questioned them. In the interviews, I wrote down just for him what the people said, as if he were right there next to me. When the conversations were printed in the magazine exactly as I had written them down, and also because of who George was, and who he was at School, I thought my take on the world was right at last, and really right.

For the very first story, George picked me up at my apartment; it felt like a date. We took the mostly empty subway—this was early afternoon—at Sixty-eighth and Lexington, downtown and over to Queens, to a small, normal-looking house on a clean, normal-looking street. I had a reporter's notebook, a brand-new tape recorder, and I felt businesslike, and proud to be riding the subway with what George sometimes called his "porous mind," and all the rest of him. His hair was longish then, pushed behind his ears, a fairly light yellow-blond. He had jeans on. George told me to take notes on the way, to have a sense of the whole time and place, the landscape, so I took notes.

The man we interviewed was a Russian-born theatre-set designer. He seemed to care about only what was ineffable, but his favorite material for sets was steel. He had dark hair, and was rather tall and soft-spoken, maybe thirty-five. He couldn't quite say where he was from in the Soviet Union, at first, though he'd been born there. That day, George asked all the questions, almost. Mostly I sat with them in the neat living room listening to the two men talk.

"What sort of place were you living in? A house? An igloo?" George asked.

"It's like a little shack, you know? Exiles, you know?" the man said.

It turned out it was somewhere south of Kazakhstan, with his parents. He came to the United States in 1979. He talked about his stage designs, the way they more or less collapsed into nothingness when the play closed, "a little memory." George later said that one main point of the story was "nowhere, collapse, obliteration, memory." Also "permanence," which is what he titled the story.

The interview took three hours, an afternoon. When we left, I was still taking notes; a tar-paper roof, a church on the street, George's big forehead. I asked him if he thought the set designer was good-looking, which was an inappropriate, non-worklike thing to say, but I said it, right outside the man's back door. "I don't have to have him like heroin in my veins," George said, in a matter-of-fact way.

That was Friday. I spent Saturday and Sunday sitting at the refectory table transcribing the tapes. I never stopped listening and typing except to eat and sleep. When I couldn't hear the words, or couldn't figure out what the man had been saying, exactly, I would rewind the tape and listen to the inaudible or incomprehensible parts over and over and over and over again, playing the tape on the stereo, my ear against the large speaker, a fuzzy-sounding whispery Russian accent coming out. The tape recorder hadn't been close enough, or the batteries were low, or the volume wasn't turned up right. But not managing to hear the dialogue, disappointing George with a flawed transcript, was completely out of the question. I can't get rid of the sound of some of those quotes—they'll never recede, they're stuck in my mind because I listened to them so many times. One of them that repeats itself from time to time is this one: "All that is solid melts into air," in a Russian accent from Marx. Another: "I think that's the whole point. Things just get forgotten." George used it for the story's last line.

.   .   .

After the trip to Queens, we didn't talk too much about that story, but on later pieces, when I did all the interviews by myself (George would think up some questions and I would write them down, like a script, and add some of my own), we would talk on the telephone afterward. The heart-racing mania I had, after an interview, to tell him what it all looked like, what I thought, what had been funny that no one would understand except him, was uncontainable until I got to a telephone. Sometimes I would call him from a pay phone in the street. I did get wildly overexcited, rhapsodic at times, about the dia-

logues I'd written down. I couldn't dislodge them from my
mind until I'd talked to George. After he'd received my package of notes and transcripts, and sat down to write the piece, he
was more or less forced to accept my take on the subject. But he
had first dibs on which quotes to use. I had thought, and then
he thought some more, and wrote about that. Our minds were
in agreement about what absurdity in its highest form was, and
beauty, and fakery and drollery, and certain forms of insanity,
and what was infinitely stupid or not. Also who the liars were.

Perhaps the truest, most thrilling part, every single time
out, was when, after writing the story, which he did fast, he
faxed it to me at School. He would call first and then I would
wait for it by the machine, and there it would be—on waxy fax
paper, off-off-white, that came out looking like a scroll. George
used the biggest font, like grade-school lettering, as if just for
me, I would imagine anyway, and it was as if the mixed-up
thing in my mind had been put in order by George. Then, after
the famously impeccable editorial procedure, the story went
into the School magazine, and, a week or so later, existed, out in
the world, for Mother and others to read.

George never read anything after the faxing ceremony. I
handled the proofs with McGrath and the checkers. He did say
once, though, that I should frame our stories, and put them all
over my room, like wallpaper.

. . .

On the morning of the Fourth of July, with fifteen transcribed
interviews about Mickey Rourke's greasy hair in the Charles
Bukowski movie *Barfly* in a clean envelope, I got on a train
and went up the Hudson to see George. He was giving a huge

party that afternoon, a giant "American" (he said) barbecue with enormous steaks cooked outside over charcoal by boy helpers, and lots of barbecue sauce. I read John O'Hara's *Pal Joey* on the train, because it was one of George's favorite books. He'd given it to me the previous week, because it's a story, told in letters from a character called Joey to his friend Ted, about not giving up, about persevering no matter what. Jean-Pierre Léaud, who was in all those Truffaut movies that Billy the Fish and I had seen in L.A., was sleeping in an armchair in the living room when I got to George's house. It was odd to see him as a living, grownup person and not a boy. In the garden, some New Englanders were pridefully talking about New England, when George, in a loyal attempt to defend my California roots, said, in one of his loudest voices, "Alison likes *hibiscus. Hibiscus!*"

It was hot and humid up at George's house. I slept upstairs in one of the back bedrooms where I spent the night whenever I went to George's. For a time, he called it Alison's Room. I took off the pink chenille bedspread that he put on the bed when he'd got the room ready for me that first Christmas, and went to sleep in the bed without anything over me.

The next, humid morning he went off to see some people and do some things in town. He was already gone when I got up. I was by myself in the stifling house, too hot and agitated to do anything, really, so what I did was I went downstairs in my Dust Bowl dress and washed all the hundreds of glasses and dishes that were piled up over every surface in his big kitchen. They were piled so high it was hard to see out the windows above the sink. The glasses were in all different shapes and sizes—no coherence—and there were wilted lettuce leaves hitched to the edges of the plates, along with dried barbecue sauce and salad dressing. There was some nice silver that was fairly black. The creamy-colored linoleum floor was dirty, too, with dirt from outdoors and with spills.

I played Elvis Presley records on an old record player in the hall, the sound turned way up high, while I did this dishwashing and cleaning—"Heartbreak Hotel" and so on, "Love Me"— and it took me all morning and afternoon. (Once, I went outside and sat on the porch overlooking the Hudson River. But I don't like big gray bodies of water all spread out like that, flattened.) The hardest part was finding free surfaces for the washed breakable things, and it occurred to me to give up now and then, but I didn't. I played a game with myself where nothing could fall over and break or you'd die, and after I'd finished, every single dirty thing was clean. I had wanted to make the kitchen perfect for him.

When George came back home, the sun was about to go down. "The sun going down," he said. "God goes to the other side of the earth and leaves you with the humans." He didn't thank me for doing the dishes, or give it any mention—he may have been embarrassed—but instead we went over the interviews on Mickey Rourke's hair. He decided the story would be called "True Hair."

After we'd done that, George drove me to the station. I finished *Pal Joey* before Poughkeepsie.

SOME GEORGE LESSONS

"The common thread is the obsession, so that—however far Person A is from Person B—you will discover or feel they are in a common story.

"There's something here you get at by discussing what people actually do. Asking questions other people don't ask and getting answers other people don't get."

. . .

Something else he said that Fourth of July, and then from time
to time: "Here's to the future, darling."

On the seventh of July, George sent me a bright-blue feather
in the mail, three and a half inches long, no note. I sometimes
thought, despite my George Lessons, that the improvisations I
had done for Wynn Handman were the very first way I learned
how to be a reporter. Now, as then, anyone would tell me anything if I above all *listened,* listened as if nothing on earth meant
more than what the other person was saying, not my dog, not
the thoughts in my own head, not even George. It was as if
talking with a person and writing down what had been said,
and having George like it even more like that, was as good as
what other people called "life" when they said "my life" in a
satisfied way.

. . .

The whole time writing Talk stories with George now looks
like a nineteen-forties movie in my head, with those calendar
pages flying off. There was a long stretch of moments when we
talked on the telephone every morning and left messages for
each other several times a day. When I walked into my apartment at night, all I cared about was the blinking light on the
machine, and then sitting down at the long table and just listening to him. Then I'd play the message again. They were so
good—they were essays, really—that I should send them back
to him, but for now I keep the tapes in a small French box
my mother gave me. For a while, I thought I'd never listen to
them again, though I liked knowing they still existed, his voice
blaring.

We did one profile together, about Richie Havens, who sang the song that went "Got those sit down, can't cry, Oh Lord I want to die blues."

"I did it for *you*," George said of the project. Havens had taken me on a little walking tour of Greenwich Village, showing me where all the old night spots used to be in the early sixties. Havens, tall and serious, and looking as sad as his singing voice sounded, told me, "Nina Simone sang right there," and he pointed to what was now a retail store. "I could have died the first time I saw her," Havens said. He was taking a drag on his Marlboro, and I could tell he meant it. It was as if Nina Simone herself were right there asking him to sing "Mississippi God Damn." It almost didn't matter that the piece as written didn't work out.

After we had done all this work together, George gave me a lecture on my message machine about Sane.

ON SANE

"The first step is to admit that you have been abused. And that's harder than it seems. I mean, it's one thing to complain and to say: 'They're fucked up.' To actually admit, you know, at times when you wanted to be given a little present, they gave you a bowl of shit instead—to actually relive the moment, or the thousands of moments, when you were secretly hoping for love and were getting something else instead. That's Step One.

"Then Step Two is to admit that that would mean that you weren't S.A.N.E." (He pronounced each letter slowly, distinctly, with pauses between them.) "How *could* you be, if that was the process going on?

"Then Step Three would be to understand that, even if you were not S.A.N.E., there were things available that were better than Sane—that you were in this whole other part of the world that was in some ways better than Sane.

"Still, you would've had to admit that 'better' was not the same as Sane Itself. And if you decided that, perhaps for passport reasons—you know, like you really need to get the passport—you had to be checked off as S.A.N.E., that you needed that, then you would have to sort of study the civil-service exam for that. Which is I think what we've been doing for the last year—sort of studying for the civil service of S.A.N.E."

"DARLING, THIS IS AMERICA"

In June of 1992, after a few years of our doing a story a month together, George got money from a movie producer to write a script about a big fire in a chicken-processing plant, which had killed a lot of people in Hamlet, North Carolina, some years earlier. George told me the fire had been an "old-fashioned disaster." He wanted me to come with him to North Carolina, to go first to a library in Charlotte, to look for clippings on the fire, and then to Hamlet, to talk to a woman who had worked in the "trim room" and a man who had been "the supervisor of the fry room." He wanted me to ask these people what a fire was like, and some other things, including "Have you been in any other fires?," "What was it like when you got up that morning?," "Where did the chickens come from?," "Are any members of your family firemen?"

We flew to Charlotte, rented a white Mazda, and had dinner with a person who gave us some general information about the big fire. Afterward, in our white car—which was to become our private sitting room—George said, "Nobody in America knows anything anymore." We never did do those interviews.

Two of the survivors talked to me from a pay phone, but what they tried to recall and the sounds of their voices were too upsetting for all of us. At any rate, the reporting trip turned into an early-summer trip to the South, a legitimate summer vacation—ushered in by George, who said, when we suddenly understood it was going to be this way, *"Darling,* this is *America."*

I can't think of when I had more fun with any human person than I had with George driving around in the South. I was too excited to look for anything wrong with it. It seemed like a real vacation to be in the car with him, hot in my Dust Bowl dress. The first morning he saw me in it in the South, he called it my Dorothea Lange dress. We saw weeping-willow trees and people in as little clothing as they could get away with. It felt safe to be with George, as if he were a Boy Scout troop leader and nothing bad or dangerous could happen to us (not getting carjacked, or held at gunpoint), and, even if it did, I'd always thought that George could kill easily, if pressed.

When he drove, his back was very straight against the seat, and he looked determined, like a general in one of those tanks with no top and a cannon in the front, the way you see them in old black-and-white war movies. He was fierce no matter what, his smallish hands on the steering wheel. Before the trip, he'd had all his hair shaved off on the sides—nineteen-fifties-like—at his local barbershop, and it made him look like Dwight David Eisenhower, whom he admired. Anyway, some of the time in the white car he didn't talk, he just drove in his ferocious way. Then I might tell him a long story about someone I particularly despised—a friend's husband, say, who never responded to what a person said; a quiet liar. "When you refuse to discuss things, you betray yourself and betray civilization,"

George said, as if what I'd told him had had to do with "civilization."

You could say what you thought was the stupidest, most humiliating thing to George and he'd listen and relate it to "civilization" or "America." In the car, I told him some story from my California childhood and he said, "You're historical in this wild way. One golden thread from the Mission." I wrote that down.

One time, his childhood friend Agatha told me, he'd said to her, "Agatha, George Washington is the *father* of our *country*." When she has imitated him saying that, we laugh so hard that both of us feel his presence take us over—it's the saddest laughter. Often I force her to say it, to feel his George Trow–ness. He is not someone you can have a normal rapport with. "Yield to it. Let it wash over you," as Chip McGrath had said. And now I did that.

For five days in that heat in the South, I was happy for the days to be just the way they were, not some other way. "Darling, we're in on a pass" was the absolute truth of the moment. That week, I liked the way George put a Martini glass down on a table in a restaurant with too much fervor, no matter where we were. I loved the way he said "Woofity Woof"—for me, in the spirit of Insane Anonymous—in between his social commentary. One time, several years earlier, he had made a tape of opera singers for me, so I would understand opera more. He titled the tape "Alison's Music," and he wrote eight pages of explanation of everything the singers were singing and what it meant. At the end of the tape—after Maria Callas singing—he'd recorded a surprise, Wilson Pickett's "In the Midnight Hour." He always knew exactly what I wanted. At the end of a silence, driving now, George said, referring to life, which I'd complained about, "The ongoingness of it is, frankly, a real problem." A little later, he said this: "The twenty-four-hour unit doesn't have to be punctuated by thousands of things."

In the mornings, we'd be in our car by eight, and stop as soon as we could where truckers stopped for breakfast. At the cash register there was always a sign: "Ask for your free trucker's discount here." Truckers would be hunched over the counter, eating and smoking. George and I would sit in a booth at the Huddle House or the Waffle House and talk while we ate. It was a euphoria, even with my dress sticking to the vinyl diner seats. George could always make up a story. (Not long ago, the poetry editor at School, Alice Quinn, said to me, and it was startling, "Why can't writers just sit down at a banquette and have interesting conversations like you and George Trow used to do?") We'd be sitting there with orange juice and waffles and empty paper containers of syrup and soft butter, and he'd say, in a Johnny Cash voice, "You want to know where we are? We're in Woofity Woof City, where every man has a dog and every woman loves her man." Then his voice got louder: "All Happy Stories—if you can't remember 'em, you can't tell 'em at Woofity Woof House. *No notes.* No More Equivocally Ambivalent Harold Brodkey."

We stayed at the Days Inn (George's choice) in Cheraw, South Carolina. George went into the front office by himself to register; I waited in the car. The rooms, which opened onto the parking lot, had pink doors, and in the morning George brought me what he'd called, the night before, George's Special Room Service, which was George knocking on my door at seven—the knock shy, not bombastic in his usual way—and bringing me a small Styrofoam cup of hot, weak coffee with Coffeemate in it. He'd got it from the front office. It was good.

He scurried back to his room, and I drank the coffee by myself, in the air-conditioning and the disinfectant stench that was all over the room, and felt happy. I was dressed already and had been waiting for him, sitting in a chair between the window and the bed.

All during the trip, I'd get up fast in the morning, no lingering or thinking. Showering, I couldn't wash my hair fast enough—the tub seemed especially slippery and vile—and then I blow-dried it any old way. In fact, I've never liked my hair better than in Cheraw, South Carolina, in June 1992, because of the fat waviness the humidity gave it. I hurried with the mascara, not too much of it, and wiped off most of my reddish lip gloss with coarse toilet paper. I had heard him get up before I did, and he was never a patient man. George took two pictures of me in my Dorothea Lange dress on that trip. In one of them, I'm leaning against the Days Inn's cheap-pink door in the morning light. In it I look really ready for something. The pink door makes me look sexy in a certain motel way. I take that picture out of the dresser drawer where I keep it only once in a while.

All week, we went back to the Cheraw Days Inn around nine-thirty, which seemed late in the South. We'd say good night outside our rooms, and when I went into my room I'd remove the huge floral bedspread and stick it in a corner of the room inside out, so the chartreuse-on-brown pattern didn't show. After I got under the worn blanket and the skimpy sheet, I read the Bible I'd found in the drawer next to the bed; I hadn't brought any books with me. I'd flip through to this or that. I did read the Twenty-third Psalm, "the valley of the shadow of death" (I liked to remember the familial hum of all the girls saying it aloud in unison in chapel at Annie Wright), and listened for sounds of George in the next room. I didn't really hear anything, but I thought I could feel him fall asleep fast, abruptly, the way he does things. Then I'd halfway go to sleep.

One afternoon after we had been driving in the heat and had gone back to the Days Inn early, George said he wanted to go for a swim. All the motels we saw had ridiculous little kidney-shaped swimming pools in front, but this one was in back, so we hadn't seen it. George went into his room and when he came out he had on a black bathing suit. It certainly wasn't a tight bathing suit, but it wasn't floppy trunks, either. I'd never seen George in a bathing suit and I felt as if it were cheating to look at him, and what if he caught me, so I tried not to, but I did watch him walk down to the pool. The way he walks is kind of a jittery march, his small blue eyes aiming at the target, chest jutting forward. He looks strong. He was doing this march in his bathing suit going down to the pool and then he turned around without a pause and came right back—I was still standing outside our rooms. The pool didn't have any water in it. This was too bad, because I was dying to follow him down there and watch him swim—he might have liked that—and now I'll have to permanently live without it.

.   .   .

George and I were constantly stopping for food in the South, in places where we saw the biggest sprayed hairdos on women. We got excited about eating. Off the highway in the middle of nowhere, deep in one of the Carolinas, we saw a discreet sign that said "The Fish Camp" in green letters. We didn't like the way it looked all that much, but we went there anyway. Inside, it was almost empty. The Fish Camp was plain, with no decoration, as if it were serving an institution: Formica tables, plate-glass windows. A large older woman in a big summer dress was talking to a short waitress in pants. We ate fried catfish with tartar sauce and George ate all his hush puppies. Afterward, our waitress—unmistakably young, and tall, and blond, in a short yellow seersucker skirt and a white blouse open at the neck— was in a lather describing the pies. She gestured in the direction of the large woman in the summer dress and told us that that woman made all the pies herself. "Bet you ain't never put anything in your mouth like these pies," she said. She had blue eyes that weren't bored or ready to pick a fight—at the moment. In a few minutes, we could see the large woman back in the kitchen, leaning over some food, stirring. Anyhow, it was true. Mine was apple, big slices in it, baked not too hard and not too soft. The crust was thick and high, like a roof over something, not flat or crisscross. George's cherry pie had the prettiest, glossiest, reddest cherries. When we were eating those pies, we were content, quiet, like animals when they eat.

Our waitress at the Fish Camp was so pretty we could have put her in the back seat of our white car and driven her to Hollywood and stardom. No matter what I said to her, she'd stare at me, holding on to her ordering pad and pencil, and pause. It was as if the way I talked was the weirdest thing she'd ever heard. Then I'd have to rephrase my question, ask again for an iced tea with lemon. At the end of the lunch, when she was tearing the check off her little pad, she and I looked at each other and broke into fairly uncontrollable giggles—we had never seen anything like each other, except in the movies— then, after about fifteen seconds, recovered. George just watched. When he and I got up to leave, the waitress said, as if she meant it, "Y'all come back and see us real soon."

George and I drove from Cheraw to Memphis, Tennessee, in about thirteen hours. We'd checked out of the Days Inn around

7 a.m. From the car, I took one last look at the pink door. I had on my dress, because he liked it so much, and he had on a turquoise button-down short-sleeved shirt and khaki trousers. I wished we could stay together forever just like that, in those clothes, in that car. But we were going to the Memphis airport.

We made a few stops along the way. I bought a cherry Popsicle next door to an Amoco station. It was really hot outside. A woman walking around the parking lot was running a can of Mountain Dew across her forehead while George got directions from a young black man at the Amoco. Two military men drove up in a red convertible. They were laughing. "Out on a spree," George said to me, and I wrote it down. Further on, we got ice-cream cones, peach and chocolate. We were eating them in a small recreation area when a little girl in a baby-blue dress with straggly honey-blond hair, barely no longer a baby, got fixated on George and was following him around and squealing with the thrill of throwing her fattish babyish arms around his pants leg. It made me nervous that he might react to the attentions of the baby girl in an inappropriate way. What if he had said, "How are you, Personality Minus?" (her parents were sitting on a bench nearby), but he didn't. He talked to her as if she were a much older girl. "That's a good-looking dress you're wearing," he said, and then I got nervous that the parents would get alarmed at his escort-at-a-cotillion mode, but they didn't do that, didn't grab the baby girl and run or anything. In fact, they thanked George for being so nice.

Back in the car, we were passing sand hills and different kinds of pine trees. We saw a completely red bird. George pointed out something by the side of the road which he said was called star leaf. It was a mass of weeds. He got out and picked one of its leaves for me and it was in the shape of a star. When we went on, I held the stem for a while, but then put it on the floor of the car, in a corner, so I wouldn't have to watch it deteriorate. We kept passing fields of very small green trees, short trees, with brown weeds in between them. George pulled over and both of us got out of the car. He took a photograph of me in my dress right in the midst of the short trees. I took one of him, too. George had those photographs made up, eight by ten, in color. I might like them better than any other inanimate thing I have.

We saw a lot of mountains and crossed a lot of rivers and admired their names: the Pee Dee, the Wateree, the French Broad, the Duck, the Big Sandy, the Wolf. The mountains were the Smokies. It was amazing to me that these places actually existed: Interstate 40, Jackson, Little Rock, Spartanburg, Knoxville, Nashville, Memphis. We had the radio on, and when the mountains didn't get in the way we heard about Billie Joe McAllister jumping off the Tallahatchie Bridge, and heard "Jailhouse Rock" (Elvis's voice in Tennessee!) and "Achy Breaky Heart," by Billy Ray Cyrus. "A special for *Alison*," George said, of it.

In the car that day, George referred to himself as Puppy Joe. I forgot what he'd been saying as soon as he said the name, because I liked it so much, it was so out of character. He only did it that one time.

George was beginning to look tired from driving, but he would never say so. The song that has the potatoes in it came on, the one that goes, "I can do the Mashed Potato, I can do the Twist, tell me baby, do you like it like this?" After the trip, I bought a tape of it: the Contours. It's in my desk, but I've never listened to it again.

By the time we got to Nashville, I was accustomed to a disinfectant smell that had been in the car from the first, and George was driving maniacally fast. We went to see the Grand

Ole Opry; it was mostly empty in the midafternoon—we went right in and sat down on the bleachers. George got up and wandered around by himself; I sat and looked at the scattered people. All the women were dressed up like Loretta Lynn.

In the airport in Memphis, George was suddenly in a hurry; he was going to be staying on a day longer, then going to Alabama. Even though I'd known of this plan from the beginning, it was awful faking the vigorous good humor required to show him it was just fine that I wasn't invited on the rest of the trip. To shove people away as he went off on his own was a character trait. "What an odd gloss we have here on Alone at Last," Renata Adler wrote in a novel. I'm quite skillful at making "Alone at Last" and its "odd gloss" manageable, even good-looking, in a public place. George walked away, leaving me sitting by myself at a small table, eating a powdered doughnut. I got on the airplane and went back to New York.

As George said once, when he thought I had missed the point, "I did it for *you.*" In my mind, I can hear him say that, "it" meaning any of it or all of it, his voice like a regular person's voice when sad. "I did it for *you.*"

At any rate, after the trip there were changes. He began referring to himself as Coldy Woldy. When he'd call and say, "*Darling.* It's Coldy Woldy—get it?," the irony was so high it was almost unreachable. There wasn't much babyishness in the delivery, despite the rhyme. He said Coldy Woldy had replaced George, and he wasn't kidding. On the telephone there was a new rule: I wasn't allowed to mention the word "Talk" to George. He broke me down one night when I transgressed this rule. But that was just one night. And in fact after we hung up I cleaned the splattered Alison from the walls and the floor fairly quickly. After all, George himself had said to me, long before, "You're tough. That's what saves us." Anyway, with George, you can't ever figure the whole thing out.

Toward the end of my knowing him, George said on the telephone, "These are the Rules of the Tunnel. You need: a flashlight, a pistol, a rope." Then he said, "The more honest you are about learning the Rules of the Tunnel, the faster you move through it." Then he said, in a semi-inaudible voice, "This is as far as human beings are allowed to go in conversation," and he hung up. He always hung up when he felt like it. He did it to everyone. He could hang up in person, too.

The actor Anthony Hopkins, who talked with me for the first Talk story I did without George, made me laugh to myself when he told me about driving across America ("Did Texas in a day") and said that driving through the Appalachians to Pittsburgh, going through the tunnels, to Beethoven's Ninth, was like *Close Encounters.* I asked him, "Were you alone?," and he said, "Yeah. Had a great time."

In that interview, too, there was an odd non sequitur, like an aside, when Hopkins said to me, "You're just like me," then went right on talking about driving across America. I wrote that down, too, for myself.

When I did a piece on Neil Diamond and called people to see if they would make fun of Neil Diamond or not, Gardner McKay called me back, from Hawaii, where he had gone to live, and sang the first three bars of "Sweet Caroline" to my answering machine.

There was a piece about a bookstore and bar on Lexington, where customers were expected to drink and read at the same time. A tall man in a pale-gray suit and a blond woman in a pink suit were sitting at the bar with Martinis and talking. "Nobody who had a brain in their body would *read* in here," the man said. There was a silence. "This is the most attractive gin mill in New York," he said, as if the fate of every metropolitan enterprise were in his hands. Then he said, "Nobody comes here to read." And, in a murmur, "It's too *dark*." I wrote down all of this verbatim. They watched me do it.

At these times, I *liked* being out of my room, on my own on the street—immersed in conversations with people, writing them down. The fragmentedness in my mind—well, I'm not going to say I was whole, exactly, as opposed to mere sprawling remnants of a human. Every single time a story was published, though, I was elated. If the weather was good, I would sit on a park bench with coffee in a paper cup and think about it— hard. Take it in. What I had done, by myself. That's what I liked.

DANGLING GIRL

Francine had been baking chicken with paprika for our lunch when a friend phoned me in Atlanta from L.A. to say that Billy the Fish had died from a heart attack. It was the week after Christmas and I had left Francine's telephone number on my answering machine in New York. Billy had had a bad flu, got scared, called a taxi in Beverly Hills, went to Cedars-Sinai by himself, and died in a bed there.

Francine squeezed half a lemon over the red-dotted chicken. Then Francine's rotund, bossy neighbor Mary Jane, a member of the Christian right, dropped by. Francine told her the death news. Mary Jane, in her fifties, wearing a shiny blue running suit with a pink checked headband in her blond hair, took over. She insisted that the three of us go into the living room, hold hands, and pray. She told us to close our eyes, but I kept mine open. ("You're not used to being around people who pray at the drop of a hat," Francine remarked later.) Mary Jane said a prayer for Billy in a Southern drawl as thick as her waistline. She prayed that Billy was in Heaven and that "we would all be together there someday."

At the end of Mary Jane's service, there was an explosion outside, which forced us to stop holding hands. The living-room lights went out. It turned out a power box had exploded, but Mary Jane said Billy the Fish was speaking to us from Heaven. She looked powerful and self-satisfied, her enormity rocking back and forth on the white sofa.

After Mary Jane made a triumphant exit, Francine and I got back into the kitchen before I had a tantrum, a certifiable fit, a breaking-down, whatever it was. I ran upstairs screaming, slammed the bedroom door. "You almost broke the doorjamb," Francine told me, after the fit had subsided. "You were mad at me because I wasn't sad enough. You said I didn't have any feelings," she said. As far as I was concerned, no one had enough feelings.

On New Year's Eve, we were upstairs in Francine's bedroom watching TV. I was cold, so Francine gave me a plaid flannel nightshirt to put over my nightgown. On one TV station, in an old black-and-white program from the fifties, Guy Lombardo and his brothers were singing, "I found a million-dollar baby in the five-and-ten-cent store." Francine got out two white masks, a shiny green noisemaker, and a tall black hat with a magenta-and-blue striped hatband. Those things just sat there in a small pile on her bed. I felt like crying. The Lombardo brothers sang a song called "Boo Hoo." Francine didn't seem to feel like crying. She never does cry.

*　*　*

When it was time for me to move out of School, Francine flew in from Atlanta to help me dismantle my School room and pack it up. I met her at the airport. It had been two and a half years since I visited her in Atlanta for Christmas. She was wearing a long white linen skirt and a black T-shirt, her blond hair tied back in that ballerina way with her habitual black velvet ribbon. The chaotic mixed-up thing in me normally vanishes when Francine is present; I become nearly invisible to myself, a consolation. It was the Fourth of July weekend and very hot, the hottest ever, but the weather didn't matter.

No one was there when we went down to School, because it was so hot and people go away over the Fourth of July. Francine hadn't been to New York in ten years, and had never seen this particular School room. We went to the storeroom and brought down stacks of flat cardboard boxes. I sat in my black chair behind the desk and watched her settle cross-legged on the unvacuumed rug, the way she used to sit and put on her mascara on Central Park West. Francine knows how to play house. She folded the pieces of cardboard until they became real boxes, ready to be filled with thousands of pieces of paper with my typing on them—drafts of published work and stacks of bulletins to Europe that were in sloppy piles all around the desk, under the desk, against three walls, and piled up in what had been an old bookcase of Harold's.

I wasn't talking, so Francine said from the floor, "Do you want to hear about the blue chicken I got for Easter when I was five?" I didn't answer. She knows when I'm slipping away. "I loved that little blue chicken," she said.

"Did it die?" I asked her. She knew the rule about No Dead Animal Stories but occasionally broke it.

"Well-l-l," she said, assembling another box, "it grew up and went somewhere else to live. I took it over to my mother's great-aunt and uncle's farm in Tennessee and left it there."

From then on, I stopped thinking about the End of School— the whole establishment was moving to abominable, tiny quarters in Times Square—and started writing down what Francine said about the blue chicken. Except for that time when Billy the Fish died, she knew how to get me out of an impending fit, had always known how to do that.

We worked hard all day long. I made a short-lived decision not to keep George's old cast-iron standing lamp that looked like a guillotine—I'd carried it over myself from our original Trow-Rose office in the previous building—but Francine said I'd be sorry if I left it behind, so now the lamp is bent over in a closet at home, like a crippled George stuck in there, where I don't see it. The Bible George had given me, with handwritten careful instructions in it about what to read and why, went under the bed.

The hardest part of disassembling the School room was deciding what to do about the three cork bulletin boards with notes from the men and other stuff all over them. Francine said they were like "a living, breathing thing." She suggested ideas about how to get them out and moved without unpinning the notes: bubble wrap, Saran wrap, making a map of where all the notes were, taking them down, then putting them up exactly the same way. Or taking photographs of the bulletin boards.

On one of the bulletin boards was an outline of my Albert Brooks profile on four legal-size pages, and things he'd said on the telephone: "Call me if you need me. Goodbye Sweetie." "The batteries are low—not in the phone, in my heart." There were also sentences other writers and editors had said about my work: "It's a real piece of writing," and so on, no names attached. The largest bulletin board had had things stuck on it in no apparent order: a piece of glossy red Christmas paper from George, along with an Italian angel he had meant to represent me, dozens of notes from him, a song he'd written for me, pieces of yellow message paper with things he'd said on them, a snapshot of Harold in aviator glasses and a jaunty red raincoat, a cassette-size album-cover photograph of the rock-and-roll singer, a black-and-white photograph I'd taken of Puppy Jane bewildered on a sidewalk, a note from Personality Plus: "Say Hello to your animals." Official printed schedules from School: my name next to Harold's and George's in the context of other real writers. George's instructions on how to report a piece about nail polish we'd done: "Is there any written material on this issue? . . . Is there *Nail Polish Monthly,* a *trade* thing? . . . In winter, does anyone think of this on the staff?" There is also a sentence from a Philip Roth novel, *Deception,* typed out by me, that goes, "If you didn't exist I'd love you like that too."

Francine and I carried shopping bags and boxes of papers down to a taxi and back to Sixty-eighth Street. It took us a long time to get them up the stairs. That night, we went to Bemelmans Bar for drinks. We looked at the dog murals on the walls, and didn't talk.

I hated it—and I mean I *hated* it—when she went back to Atlanta the next morning.

I returned to my office at night, alone with a boom box for courage, and went on packing by myself. I listened to the oldies radio station, turned it up loud. On the top of one empty box I wrote down some of the names of the songs, so I could laugh when I unpacked it. "I Just Called to Say I Love You" was one. Most of the time, though, I just sat at the desk listening to the radio. Sometimes I looked at the photographs of Harold and George on the walls. Other times I put my head on the desk sideways, my cheek on the papers.

My papers and notebooks were piled so high on the large desk that, though I planned, night after night, with the courage radio on, to attack them and put them in boxes, I didn't.

Finally, a friend who had nothing to do with School met me in the lobby of the building at 8:30 a.m. on a Sunday morning. He brought a red truck and a strong Norwegian friend for help. He wasn't pleased when he walked in and saw the desk.

"I can't do anything about it," I said.

Right then, he pushed everything on the desktop into a large box Francine had assembled that sat beside it. He did this with one long arm, a firm, sweeping gesture. Then he put the rest of the papers from the bookshelves and the floor into more boxes.

I did have to remove everything from the largest bulletin board and put it all into a folder—no map, no photograph. It was as serious a fragmentation of what had actually been my life as when Mother sharpened my pencils. I carried the bulletin board and the folder to the truck myself. The two smaller bulletin boards could be kept intact. I waited for the wind to die before I took them down to the street and made sure nothing fell off or was squashed, and in the truck I put a blanket over them. The smaller boards were easy to hold against my chest when I carried them out. Nothing did fall off.

In the end, when I left the office for good, Renata came with me. I had kept the photographs of Harold and George on the walls until that last minute. Renata took them off the walls for me. She did it fast, passing them to me, and I put them in a black shopping bag. On the ride down in the elevator, the photograph of Harold's face, old, a cigarette dangling from his mouth, was looking up from the bag when I looked down into it. He was definitely dead.

·   ·   ·

It was three years before that that Harold had withdrawn into sickness and then had died. His death was a terrible surprise. It wasn't in his character to die.

When I first knew him and every day felt dangerous because at some point he *might* die, he said that it wouldn't "matter" to me if he died, because I could still read him, the same way I had before I met him. He added that he wasn't a person anyway.

Howard and I had lunch in a Japanese restaurant not long after Harold died. The best thing Howard said was "We'll miss the dialogue but it won't be that different, dead or alive." He made a drawing—he was always making drawings—of a box, with measurements. He did it on a white napkin in black ink. When he handed the drawing to me, he explained that it was the box with Harold's ashes in it, and we laughed. The napkin is folded neatly in the drawer next to my bed. I think we buried Harold that day, more or less, in a nice way. There was nothing cold about it, exactly. I think Harold would have thought it was funny. Maybe not.

.   .   .

A woman I know who was sick and thought she'd never get well went to stay with a man she knew in Puerto Vallarta, Mexico. The man gave her a present, a canary. The woman took very good care of the canary, watched over it from every angle nearly all day long. The canary sang for her at an affectionate pitch and she attended to its every comfort: never an unsmooth yellow feather on its body, the most refined birdseed. Then the woman had to take a sudden trip to Mexico City, leaving the man to look after the canary, and also a cat.

While she was away, the cat slit the canary's throat. The man was nearly undone, but not to the point of inaction. He found the only person in Puerto Vallarta who knew precisely how to repair a canary's torn throat, and the wound healed; the canary recovered, and seemed like a brand-new canary, as happy as it had been in the first place, except that it was silent. The man was distressed that the canary was unable to sing, but when the woman returned from Mexico City and sat by its cage for part of an afternoon, the canary sang for her. It still sings, but only if she's right there.

I refuse to be the dejected little girl who says no one ever gives her a diamond, or a canary. After all: Harold. George. I got given a canary twice.

Whenever I get off an airplane at the San Francisco airport and my sister meets me in her car and we drive down to Atherton, I always think this: The sky is terrible here, even when it's blue; I hate it. I hate the *air;* it feels thin. In Atherton at Mother's house there are those trees I hate; dark trees with too many leaves. The thing I hate most, driving down there, is the SOUTH SAN FRANCISCO sign, white lettering on a brown hillside; a reliable symbol of psychic disintegration and the fear of never getting out of California.

I see the sign, and the whole *famille horride* is suddenly in the car—including my father, who's been dead for twenty years. My sister drives past it—SOUTH SAN FRANCISCO—but in my mind she pulls off, they all get out, and they drag me up the hill, to where that enormous lettering is, and semi-inter me in the dirt under the big sign. My sister might be driving along placidly and saying, "Mother has always looked perfect no matter what time of day it is, from the first thing in the morning to being glamorous when she goes to bed." But there we are: less than an hour from Atherton, attending my burial. This is one reason I don't like to take Puppy Jane on a trip to see Mother. Jane is safer in a cage at the vet's on Sixty-fourth Street in New York City.

I wanted to interview Mother using my tape recorder. I wanted her personality, the essence of her oddness, her particular rhythm, on transcribable tape, where it would mean something to me. Mother and I aren't comfortable when we see each other in person, and anyway there are times I don't care for real live life. I wanted her to talk, and she did, about her little boarding school in Paris, Residence Ribera, 37 Rue Ribera, Paris 16, in the twenties, and her dresses made by Vionnet ("I was in school in Europe between the wars, by the way"), about the dogs in her life, and her Grand Tour of Europe at eighteen ("There were footmen and drivers"). "I could have married a man I met at the Lido in Venice, but he was short and not particularly attractive," she said. "He wasn't bad-looking, but I like tall men."

Mother talked deliriously about having taken the train from San Francisco to Chicago, from Chicago to New York. "The Overland Limited," she said. "That's a fact. It's nothing I dreamed up."

This is what my mother said about my sister: "She deals rigidly with trivia. If she's talking about a board meeting she attended, at that moment I can't ask her what the cat eats."

When I interviewed her, Mother was wearing a pale-pink silk robe over her bed jacket and nightgown, and a long silk scarf, and pearl earrings. It was seven-thirty in the morning. She looked at the big old clock above the table, then at her watch. "The clocks are all a little bit sick," she said. Mother talked for an hour and a half. She has stories. The one about her maternal grandfather getting trampled to death by a bull on the ferry commuting to San Francisco from Oakland is good. His entire self was unrecognizable. The police had only a wrist-watch to take back to his wife. Mother tells it like a real reporter.

At nine o'clock this particular morning, the new maid, somewhat young, from Honduras, was in the kitchen with us. Mother was telling her about recipes for dog food, and the maid was standing by the kitchen sink with a freshly cut pile of full-blossomed orange branches and dark-pink roses under her hands. She'd just come in with them, and she put them in water while Mother went on to discuss picking flowers with her, and whether or not the roses were as good as they used to be, and fertilizer, and the gardener, and the sun.

"The trees are so tall they keep the sun off the roses," Mother said. "It used to be too bright and now it's too dark, because of the trees."

Out the window in Mother's kitchen in Atherton—it's a glass house—is a gigantic white-oak tree, which makes everything outside look dark. My mother says it has a disease. For all her wittiness and charm, she tends often to throw in a threatening, sad thing like that; a tree having a disease. You always know it's coming; a bad thing. According to Mother, the tree is two thousand years old, and adds fifty thousand dollars to the value of the property. Everything is dark out there, even at noon. The swimming pool is dark, too; she had it painted dark green so it would look like a lake or something—she loathes blue swimming pools, thinks they're cheap, like Los Angeles. The pool is so dark a green that it's like the middle of a lake at night where no one's around if you fall in.

It would surely have been a moment for Daddy to proclaim "Nonsense!" To drown out their talking I began chanting,

192 / BETTER THAN SANE

"Puppy *Sue,* Puppy *Sue*. Puppy, Puppy *Suuuue,*" a lullaby for myself. The maid gave me a series of "Be nice to your mother" looks.

That night, while Mother and I were having dessert—this frozen strawberry thing she makes from scratch, nothing's better—Francine called, and I told her about the dessert. Francine said to ask Mother how she made it, so I handed the receiver to Mother, who said to Francine, though they hadn't spoken in years, "Hello, dear, the banana has to be very ripe and tired. The big trick is the tired banana. It has to be very tired or it won't work."

"Remember when Daddy thought Francine was so pretty?" I said to Mother, who was still talking to Francine about mashing the strawberries and the tired banana. It had been a night in Los Angeles in 1970 when Francine was all dressed up for something—I forget what—and she had on this long, sleek, close-fitting white Jean Harlow dress. We were in my parents' hotel room at the Bel-Air, and my father was watching Francine as she sat in an armchair or walked across the room and back to the armchair, never not watching her. "She wasn't just pretty. She was the most beautiful little girl he ever saw," Mother said to me now. Then she went on further to Francine about the consistency of the tired banana and the strawberries, the exact amount of sugar, how long it takes to freeze.

Now my sister comes into the house followed by her old white, medium-big dog, Cleo, named after her former psychiatrist. Mother and she talk about salmon. A long discussion about salmon. It's astounding how, after four decades or so, almost half a century, they can still talk and talk about food; gossip about it, plan it, never get tired of it or show a single sign of boredom.

. . .

When I went to Atherton for my mother's ninetieth birthday, five years ago in June, I took along Puppy Jane. I had to kind of shove her into a black nylon dog-carrying case I'd bought for the trip, and there she was, stuffed under the airplane seat in front of me for five and a half hours, all the way to San Francisco. The one time I got up to go to the bathroom, the woman who was sitting next to me said Jane wailed the whole time, and I'd heard her, on my walk back down the aisle, but once I was seated again, my feet in front of the black case, she was fine.

My sister met us at the gate—she'd never seen Puppy Jane before—and it was all so exciting: Puppy in her silky-clean white fur (she's a Maltese), ecstatically panting, my sister in her stylish black suit, pearls, other jewelry. She always dresses like a grown woman—always did—which may be one reason she used to call me a "girl-person." My sister said some high-pitched words of praise to Puppy Jane and Puppy Jane wriggled out of my arms and into hers, which made me uneasy. We walked to the car, got in, and Jane was jumping all over, enthusiasm in her eyes. We got to Atherton, and to make it seem more as if I was casually in charge, though I was nervous about it, I took her leash off as we entered Mother's house. When I put her down, however, she raced past my sister down the hallway with the stone floors and the Persian rugs, and straight out the open glass doors in back, non-stop, and landed right in the dark-green swimming pool, a small splash. All I can remember is standing there watching and Puppy paddling madly, head held high. She'd never been in any body of water before, and I froze, my heart sinking faster than the time she'd actually take to drown. But my sister, in her black suit and jewelry, pushed me aside, not too aggressively, went out and leaned way over the edge of the pool, nearly falling in, and with no overt display of panic rescued my dog, who hadn't realized that anything bad had happened to her.

My sister handed her to me—she was all wet, with visible pink skin and an extraordinarily slim underbelly showing under the bright sun. Mother had met Puppy Jane in New York, when she'd stopped off to see me after one of her trips to Washington or Paris and I'd brought Jane to the Mayfair Regent, where Mother was staying. Now Mother and her dogs—a black standard poodle and a gray smaller one—caught up with us out by the dark pool. Mother handed me a striped beach towel that had been lying folded on a chair, so I could wrap Jane in it. I took her back into the house and dried her in Daddy's old bathroom with a 1,500-watt hair dryer. I don't think my mother and sister thought of the incident the way I imagined they did: "Alison can't even take care of a puppy." "I told you so." No one mentioned the near crisis again, though I kept expecting them to.

Mother wasn't used to having such a small dog around, and I was constantly afraid she might step on Jane. There were a few close calls, so I asked my friend Barbara, an efficient being I'd known since kindergarten, to come over and drive me to a pet store in Menlo Park, where I bought some bells to put on Jane's collar so Mother would hear her; Jane's paw-sounds on floors aren't loud.

Whenever I left a room in Mother's house, Puppy Jane would follow me, bells jingling, rather than staying with Mother or my sister, even when they called her. My sister said I was somehow forcing her to ignore them, but I wasn't. Jane got along nicely with my sister's white dog, and with Mother's gray and black dogs, and with a yellow Persian cat Mother had. I took pictures of those animals together in the garden. A picture of Puppy Jane sitting alone by the pool, as if she were Bardot in Cannes (as photographed by Andy Warhol, Personality Plus remarked), is framed on my round table in New York.

One afternoon there was a birthday party for Mother in the garden, and a lot of people came. As the first guests were arriving, I picked up Puppy Jane to carry her out to the party, but my sister yelled at me, in our father's grand tradition, *"You take your little dog and go to your room!"* She sounded remarkably like the Wicked Witch in *The Wizard of Oz*—a movie I've never been able to sit through, because I'm too afraid the dog will die. It was one of our most irrational fights. I didn't go to my room, however, and after both of us had screamed some more, I kept Jane in my arms the entire afternoon. That way, I didn't have to talk to anyone much, except about the dog.

. . .

Mother being interviewed was cheerful, whatever she was talking about. She talked about how, in the early nineteen-hundreds, her family, the Phillipses, had a country house at Arroyo Grande in San Luis Obispo County, 2,241 acres. They had horses and carriages, and cows. It was in the middle of nowhere, and the Phillipses had bought it for fifty cents an acre from the Mexican government before California was a state; the family owned this property for a hundred and two years and sold it in 1915 for $17.5 million. Mother had told us that story ten billion times, but this was the first time I actually listened to it. Later she showed me the leather-bound newspaper stories about her family's history, Mother and I sitting on the bench at the foot of her bed, my sister leaning against an old Venetian desk, looking out the glass doors, at gardenias blooming like mad, not listening. "Would you please write down in your little notebook that you both drive me crazy," my mother says, sort of out of the blue, but not really.

Fitel Phillips, Mother's great-grandfather, who was born in 1825 in Kemper, Prussia, sailed in 1850 on the steamer Columbo, arriving on the East Coast on the seventh of July. Mother giddily tells the part about Fitel Phillips buying a mule and riding it across the Isthmus of Panama. There are photographs of Alaska in the collection of newspaper stories: a team of sled dogs, a house made of logs. Mother makes it very clear that her great-grandfather didn't dig for gold himself during the gold rush but, rather, did business with those who had already found it, which was a good idea, as he later acquired business property at Ellis and Mason Streets in San Francisco, and a residence on the corner of Sutter and Stockton. He kept a diary in ornate penmanship, black ink with fine swirls, about who died in his family and when. I read that, too. This man made it possible for my mother and my sister and me to exist here in Northern California; to talk about salmon, schizophrenia, roses with aphids, and dog food; and to be semi-attuned to the unreason in one another. "It's harder in a sunny place," George Trow said once about my California childhood. Fitel Phillips also made it possible for me to leave.

"What did we put the loquat leaves in, Tita?" Mother says to the maid. "Oh, did Tom pick some for you to put in there? Oh? He did?" Tom is the tree man. He still worships Mother. He's schizophrenic, as Mother doesn't mind saying. ("If he doesn't take the medication he'll be dead.") I can tell he still worships her from the way they talk about the roses.

"We are having string beans with salmon for lunch and little potatoes," my mother says to my sister. "I actually did the stringing on these beans. For instance, I missed one."

"You snap off the ends," my sister says.

"It was exercise," my mother says. Now she's making a sauce for the salmon we'll have for lunch. "I don't like to *taste* the mayonnaise," she says. "There was parsley in the original dosage," she goes on. It's true that my mother is the best cook in Western civilization and that all her maids learned to cook the way she does.

"I love these Japanese cucumbers," my sister says. "I don't think anyone buys them. There are only three or four in a tray." Mother and my sister talk about bulbs for the halogen lights outside near the front door, in an inner courtyard, where the azaleas and the trumpet vine are. While they are talking, I am saying, "Puppy *Sue,* Puppy *Sue,* Puppy Puppy *Suuuue.*" They ignore me. They're used to it.

Near the back of the kitchen there's a small pantry. There are cupboards with rice and cereal in them, but mainly there's so much food for the animals. There are bowls of dry cat food and dog food on the floor, cans of Fancy Feast piled high on the counter by two stainless-steel sinks, a recipe on an index card for Cooked Turkey for Animals on top of a lot of other food for animals and special recipes for dogs. Recently when I asked my mother to give one single example of Daddy's "kindness," she said after a long minute's pause, "He was very good to the dogs when they were sick. He went to the vet every day to give Boots fresh meat."

Noel, the black poodle my sister got on Christmas Day when she was thirteen, didn't like me very much, and, years later, neither did Mother's first gray poodle, Follie. Follie paid no attention to me whatsoever, very little eye contact. Although I was nice to them both, and hoped they would come see me in my room, they didn't. Mother got Follie when I was already thirty or so, and up visiting from Los Angeles. I made up names for her: Whip-a-Puppy and Nobody Likes You Puppy Sue. I would go outside at dinnertime and call her: "*Here,* Nobody Likes You Puppy Sue!"

Mother, mostly without thinking, would sometimes look down at Follie and say, and it soon became a refrain of hers, "Nobody Likes You Puppy Sue."

•   •   •

Fall before last, on one of those days that are almost too bright in Northern California—it was October—my sister and I drove from Mother's house in Atherton to Nita's house in Richmond, in the East Bay. I was all excited to see Nita, and nervous she'd still be mad at me. Juanita Johnson.

The apartment complex was in compact one-story sections built in the fifties or sixties, tidy, painted an uncomplicated beige. There was a blue parakeet in a cage hanging in a window in the apartment next to Nita's. Nita came out of her front door as we were walking toward it. It was a wonder to see her again—Nita!—and she looked just about exactly the same. It didn't count for much that her hair was shorter and without the former pomade stuff combed into it. The first thing she said was "Not *you,* Alis'. Not *you.*" She shook her head and laughed. I said it was nice to see her, and really weird, too, and that I didn't know where I was or how old I was.

Nita said, "You talk more, Alis'. Uh-*huh,* uh-*huh,*" and she nodded, as if still confirming to herself that what she'd just observed was accurate. Inside, every inch of the apartment had something on it, but all the things were in their places, and immaculate. On the back patio there were as many orchids as a person could fit on a smallish table, and little plants in pots all over the ground. The whole time, I was wondering which songs were in an old rack of 45s near the front door, but I never did ask.

Nita has a good figure still. She's always had men, and she has one now, she said, but he lives somewhere else. She was wearing a close-fitting floral-patterned cotton top, tan pedal pushers, camel-colored sandals, and salmon-pinkish fingernail polish. One thing different about the way Nita looked was she wasn't wearing those thick glasses, or any glasses at all—at some point after she had stopped working at our house, my father had arranged to have her crossed eye fixed.

The main focus in her living room was a formal wooden table, which was set for eight: polished flatware, wine goblets with folded pink cloth napkins inside them, white dinner plates with gold rims. Mother had taught Nita to set the table like that, except the napkins hadn't been in the glasses. On a side table there was candy in a dish, too, sort of the way Mother did it. We didn't sit at the dining table—it was like a piece of art unto itself, the whole thing set like that. We admired it silently.

She said now, "What happened to your curly hair, Alis'? You used to have *curly* hair." It was as if she were actually disappointed in my hair. Then she came over and stood in front of me, crossed her arms, and said, "I haven't seen you since you was *impossible.*" She shook her head and laughed.

Nita directed most of her conversation to my sister, but looked hard at me now and then. "Alis', she was a bad girl," she said to my sister. "She kept a dirty room. She was so independent she never would keep her room clean. She wouldn't. You couldn't touch nothin', 'cause it was so dirty in there. Your clothes was on the floor, your slips and panties was on the floor. Uh-*huh*. Uh-*huh*. You had pets in there. There was a skunk up there, guinea pigs. Remember the time you got a sick dog in there? Your father was screamin'. You said you would run away from home."

"Why didn't Mother make me clean up my room?" I asked. I didn't say that the skunk was actually a black-and-white cat we called Skunk. On Monday mornings, Skunk would wait for Nita to step off the bus, and walk with her back to our house.

"You was so difficult you'd probably knock her down the stairs," Nita said, and she laughed hard to herself.

My sister asked Nita about a friend of Mother's who'd been something of a bully.

"I don't know why your mother care for her so much," Nita said with disgust. "Your father got her out of the house. He said, 'You get out of this house and don't you ever come back.' It was at the dinner table and he was hollerin'. I was cryin' and your mother was cryin'." Nita paused and then said, "We can tell these stories 'cause we're ladies now."

"Why was I mean to you, do you think?"

"You just didn't like me, Alis'," she said matter-of-factly. "You was that kind of person."

To my sister a little later Nita said, "Your mother act like she didn't like you. She liked Alis' better. You couldn't go to school without makin' your bed. You got married and your mother *still* was bossin' you."

"Did you ever like me?" I asked her then.

"I didn't like you, *period*. You was too *dirty*. You had guinea pigs and skunks up there. Kay"—the Japanese maid—"took care of your room. Your sister was a nice, neat person."

"Did you like my father?"

"No. He was nice and he was not nice. He would holler. Your mother was in love with him—women like tall men—so she took that.

"Alis', remember you would eat the dog food? You and Squirrel, one Saturday night, I had cooked the dog food for Noel, horse meat, ground up, and y'all ate it—the dog food! That was one Saturday night."

"What *else* did you think of my father?" I asked her.

"He *was* cruel. Very cruel. You two would laugh at the dinner table—you would make your father so angry. Oh, he was very cruel. Oh, he was *very* angry. I don't think he liked children. Everything Alis' would do he would yell at her. He never did want no children, but your mother did. Y'all didn't talk none at the dinner table. Y'all eat."

My sister started to have out-of-control giggles. "Remember the carving fights?" she said to Nita. Our family used to have great pieces of roasted meat for dinner, which required carving: leg of lamb or some big cut of beef. All three of us, I could tell, were picturing the six-rib roast on the large silver platter with enormous silver carving utensils, my father yelling that the knives weren't sharp enough. He wasn't a good carver, to tell the truth, though he persisted. "He'd slam the two knives down," Nita said, "and wouldn't do nothin'. Oh, he was terrible. Your mother made it through. He was still hollerin'. Uh-huh. Uh-huh."

"Alis', she would take her food upstairs," Nita said to my sister as if I weren't there. "You would watch me cook, 'cause you wanted to get married. They was mean to you when you married. I said, 'The child has to marry someone.'"

My sister asked Nita if she thought Mother should have divorced my father.

"All she have to do is go to Reno and go back home. Oh, *that house was a crazy house. Everybody was doin' their own thing. Nobody was happy in that house. There was no happiness there.* At breakfast he'd come down with the devil in him. He'd start to talk about the black people. I start to talk about the Jew people. When Kennedy got shot they say a black man kill him. I said it could have been a Jew kill him. And it turned out a Jew killed him." She was sitting in the chair and she just looked from my sister to me and said again, this time in a firm but quieter voice, "It was a crazy house and I don't know how you and Alis' lived there. It was a *crazy* house."

Nita got quieter then. My sister and I didn't say anything. "Your mother said your father never did buy you nothin' *ever.*"

Then Nita looked right at me. She said, "You *hated* your mother, you *hated* your father, and you hated me. Alis', you were independent. You didn't like me to fix nothin'." Then she imitated me: "I fix my *own* dinner." She clapped her hands together hard and leaned over in her chair, laughing hard. "You was just a person who wanted to be by yourself, you didn't want nobody to do nothin' for you. You'd stay in your room until your mother made you bring the dishes down. Uh-huh."

Nita got back onto my old room—she couldn't seem to stop talking about how dirty I kept it.

"Did you think I would ever get married?" I asked her.

"No. I never did think you would ever get married. *Never.* You never did care about nothin' like that. If you were married you wouldn't know what to do. You was a lonely person. All the time you would stay in your room. You would only come down for dinner."

I asked her about niceness—who had been nice—and she mentioned a few of my friends, then she suddenly said, "There was one person who wasn't nice to you. Your father. He was *real* mean and your mother was *so* nice. When your mother's mother passed, he took himself on a trip around the world. Your father never did anything for any of you. Your sister was really my chile. She was a kindheart. Your mother wasn't nice to your sister. I took her for my chile and I lied for her. I sneaked in there and cleaned up her room."

"Why did he tell me I was crazy?" I asked.

"You were going to do what you want, regardless, and that's what he didn't like. That was a house that was not together. Everybody was by itself."

When my sister and I got up to leave, I felt sad but didn't show it. We were all polite, said thank you and embraced and laughed and promised it wouldn't be so long until the next time. I said to Nita, "I keep my room pretty clean now." There was a long pause. "You don't believe me, do you?"

"Not too much, Alis'."

"How did you think I would turn out?"

"Live by yourself and be grouchy," she said. "Uh-huh. Uh-huh."

"What do you like to do best these days?" I asked her.

"The only thing I like is to be clean and to pay my bills."

Nita waited outside her front door while we walked to the car, about half a block down the street. We turned, and everyone waved. We were already in the car when Nita came running after us. Nita stood there on the sidewalk, leaning forward a little with her hands behind her back, just the way she used to do in her starched white uniform in our kitchen in Palo Alto. I rolled down my window and she said, not quite in a whisper but just to me, "Alis', it was a crazy house. That's all."

ROOM, WITH VIEW

I've liked being in my room my whole life. In Palo Alto, my room—the bedroom (with the door shut) and the veranda—had everything in one place: the wisteria, the bougainvillea, my yellow cat, the pencils; the black-and-white TV; the thoughts about the humans without the humans. Little jolts of safety in a sealed place.

This room here, on East Sixty-eighth Street in New York, is my whole self now, I sometimes think. "A little island you'd never want to get off of," a new friend said, seeing it. I've put the School room back together right inside this room. The bulletin boards with the sacred notes on them are hanging in the hallway now; this way, as I pass back and forth to the kitchen I can see them and read them if I want to. "All of us who love you are your cover," and I'm still covered, in a manner of speaking.

There's a framed envelope addressed to Harold on the wall next to the mirror. In his handwriting is a birthday greeting he made for Puppy Jane. He made a pencil drawing of Puppy Jane jumping over a wastepaper basket. Next to the drawing he wrote, in pencil, "Puppy leaps over a large wastepaper basket."

The day before he made the birthday card for Puppy—I'd brought her into the office and introduced her to some writers and editors—I was carrying her under her front legs, her dog ankles were crossed, and Harold said, "She should be wearing a skirt."

I especially like the view from the bed. In the morning, when there's sun, the light comes in through the trees on the street and the colored leaded glass. I like to be with the cat and the dog—sun on the animals—and look at all this without thoughts. Or I pull up a chair next to the windows and it's like having breakfast in a tree house. A few not-hostile-seeming birds are sitting in the trees, or, if they've found food, they eat together on the sidewalk. Around noon, the colored-glass light shines on the opposite wall, rose-colored, in rectangles, as if the plain morning light weren't good enough. Harold said I was "already utterly ruined," but one certainty is that there's no such thing as ruination here.

I like to stay in bed because the sheets are soft. They're worn thin, the threads baby-soft from being washed over and over again. I like to open the Chinese-laundry package, brown wrapping with string, and see that the sheets survived, again, all the whirling, thrashing, and writhing around in a professional washer and dryer, the pressing with steam. I still like night-gowns. I have more of them: a white one from Brazil, like a Ginger Rogers dancing dress, except for the small blue dots. The thought of having clothes, street clothes, next to my skin instead of this nightgown, these sheets, a silky dog, a cat, is nearly unthinkable, more often than not. In the morning, it takes me a long time to stand up and face just plain air, the abrupt water from the shower, the inevitable coarseness of a towel. I hate terry cloth (Harold said he did, too), so I can't stand drying myself. I have mental fortitude, though, and I do it anyway.

Toast got old, then she got sick and sicker. I was shying away from what I would have to do about Toast. A woman at School, who's normally reliably droll in a sharp-witted way, wasn't when she told me I had to think of *Toast*. I hate the expressions for what was going to happen next: she wasn't going to be "put to sleep," she was going to die. But I made an appointment for her death at noon, sun right up there in the sky. I had to drag Toast out from under the bed, put her in a cat suitcase, and carry her four blocks down Park Avenue.

It was cold. A maternal veterinarian with long blond hair had me bring Toast to an examination room. On the stainless-steel examining table, still in her case, Toast was mostly limp. The blond woman had two rings on her wedding finger, a normal gold band and a ring with a pear-shaped diamond in it. Even though Toast was going to die within minutes, I thought about how this veterinarian must be a nice wife and all that—a nice mother, I really mean. She lifted Toast out of the case carefully, cradled her, holding her up, and forward a bit, as if saying, "It's O.K.," so I could say my goodbye. I leaned to kiss Toast on her mouth. I could feel her thin, warm lips, and then the blond woman took her upstairs. I dashed out the side exit that mourners were supposed to use, forgetting my coat.

Puppy Jane is twelve. Francie Caroline Cederquist, my kitten, has small eyes, a straight nose, and high cheekbones. She's plain, that's the main thing, with very short, pale-calico fur. I waited nearly a year before I got Francie Caroline Cederquist, around Thanksgiving two years ago. Over the telephone to Atlanta that night, I told Francine that the still nameless kitten looked exactly the way the actress Peggy Ann Garner had looked when she played Francie in the movie *A Tree Grows in Brooklyn,* if Peggy Ann Garner had had a crewcut. That's why we named her Francie, right then, immediately. Caroline had been Toast's name on her A.S.P.C.A. certificate. Cederquist is for Dr. Cederquist, because he died not long after Toast died.

Francie Caroline Cederquist likes to kiss back. When I'm on the bed, she sits on my chest and kisses me on the mouth with her rough cat tongue. The tongue gets rougher as she gets bigger, I've noticed. Sometimes the kissing can be disconcerting. If I want to sleep, I remove Francie from my chest and zip her up in a small black mesh bag, A.S.P.C.A. approved, what a friend calls the No-Kissing Pen. Puppy Jane will give the bag a worrisome look.

In this room there's everything. There is even family tradition. My mother said her mother told her a house had to have "candy, fresh flowers, and a freshly baked cake." I have a small silver dish with Jordan almonds in it, another with chocolates wrapped in shiny foil stamped with pansies. People who come to visit perhaps somehow feel that they shouldn't eat the candy, and they somehow don't. Right now there are roses, apricot and snapdragon pink, on the round table with the pictures of the animals on it. One time, I baked a fresh chocolate cake for Harold, spelling out his name on the icing with candied violets. The pastel candies and the flowers make the place look "like Easter all year round," a young woman visiting remarked recently. She said George's postcard with its five palm trees against a blue sky, the way it hung above the bed, suggested an icon of Jesus. So there you are, George, the highest form of reciprocal salvation anyone could offer.

I've reorganized the closets to make room for some of the boxes from School. George's silk necktie, off-white with a pattern of burgundy diamonds, hangs over the rod in there. He didn't give it to me, he left it there, the way people do. Often the necktie slips off the rod and I find it—an unnerving surprise—on the floor. I toss it helter-skelter back over the rod. It'll fall again.

There was a Tuesday one January when I took the train up to the country to have lunch with George. We'd have lunch in the same restaurant, to talk about work ideas, then drive around, and I'd take an early train back, and look at the Hudson River or read. This January day when I got off at his station, I was nervously waiting for him there when he came running toward me on the platform, really running, not wanting me to think he wasn't there on time; and he was smiling, broadly. There was this second when he stopped right in front of me; a quarter of a second of embarrassment, as if he'd caught himself, and I'd caught him, too, showing uncontrolled excitement to see me. I like to think about him running toward me like that.

The very last weekend I spent up at George's house, he said to me, "Try to see what the focus is. No, don't *try*. *See* it: the *focus*. Are you listening? It's been twenty-five years of extended appealing youth and possibility"—he meant for both of us. "Now it's almost over, and I mean *now*." He said that in his upstate kitchen, at a round table with a cloth over it, where we were having breakfast. I didn't write it down; it's engraved in my brain.

I had to clear things off the refectory table so I could work here. A photograph of me and Billy the Fish sitting in a good French chair at Monique's apartment in West Hollywood went into my grandmother's old quilted sewing box, which came off the worktable and is on the bureau now. The spools of thread inside it are from L.A., where Monique bought them for me. The sewing box makes a nice casket for youth (*jeunesse*) and sadness (*tristesse*). It sits next to a photograph of Mother from 1917, wearing a smocked dress and standing outside a summer house in Marin County—which at least makes California sense: "One golden thread from the Mission." I left on the refectory table a handmade jar for pencils, glazed blue, that dear Europe had abandoned in his office at School when he moved out, in one of the waves of resignations some years ago. Now the blue-glazed jar is getting practical use. I don't think about him every time I look at it, as I don't necessarily think about George or Jesus or the palm trees when I'm in my room, because yearning and having nothing are the same thing. And, as I said, there's everything in this room.

I call Mother more now than I used to, working in my room. Here is part of a telephone conversation we had last week. I wrote it down. Mother's voice is still fairly strong, but she doesn't talk as fast as she used to. She is ninety-five.

"Well, hello. How do you do?" Mother said first, in "Miss Jones, I presume" mode. She was waiting for the next nurse to take over. She has three nurses. She said she wanted to go to her bedroom to find the *Times* piece about Burt Lancaster, so she could read it to me. She said she could use her cane to get there. Then she said she shouldn't do that, because she might fall down.

"The doctor said it would be very bad if I fell down." Then she said, as if with good cheer, "I think it would be sort of a good idea, don't you?"

I said I didn't think so, no.

"I think I should be put in a garbage can," Mother said. "I've asked Belinda to put me in a garbage can, but she won't. Would you put me in a garbage can?"

I said no, I didn't think so. She was considering a particular garbage can, she said, the one by the beauty parlor where she gets her hair done, in Menlo Park.

"What does it look like?" I asked her.

"A great big blue thing about six feet high on a wooden base. It says something—I can't remember what—in English and in Spanish. California's population is definitely Latino now. There're more Latinos than whatever it is we are. I don't know what it says. I'll know next Thursday when I get my hair done."

"What do you think about Daddy?" I asked.

"He was a wonderful dancer," she said.

"What about love?"

"Oh, yes," Mother said, "that would have been nice. His last words to me in the nursing home were 'I hate you.'"

"Why did he say that?"

"Because I had the nerve to be alive and well, I think." Then she started going on the way she always has, about Yale and all his degrees: the B.A., the M.A., the Ph.D., the M.D., the D.P.H.

"I don't care," I said, for the first time ever.

"Well, I don't either, as a matter of fact," Mother said, also for the first time.

"My sister doesn't have a sense of humor," I said, as if to follow up.

"She doesn't. Now, that's true," Mother said.

"But why doesn't she have a sense of humor?"

"I don't know. I haven't mentioned it and I recommend that you don't."

"But why doesn't she have a sense of humor?"

"I don't know," Mother said. "Why don't you have blonder hair?"

. . .

Mother has acquired immortality. My sister bought it for her. There are forty-eight bronze bells on the fourteenth floor of Hoover Tower at Stanford University. The heaviest bell weighs 2.5 tons. A much smaller bell, A-sharp, weighing in at twenty-five pounds, is engraved like this: "In Honor of Alice Phillips Rose." "In honor of" suggests that the honoree, Mother, in this case, is still alive, though the bell will ring for her when she is dead, of course. Not just anyone can have a bell at Hoover. Mother did important work there. She discovered papers in the archives about eight hundred children who were hidden, along with their teachers, in Petrograd during the Russian Revolution. At some point the teachers ran off, leaving the children alone. After the war, the children were put on a freighter and sent to Japan, where the freighter was renovated, or whatever, with bunk beds and other comforts, and sent, along with the children, back home to Russia. Mother herself was sent to Russia, with a small group, about an official matter in the dead of winter, when she was eighty. I have snapshots of Mother, small in a great big coat, a furry Russian hat covering her head, smiling on a street in Moscow, snow all over the ground.

In any case, no matter what, Mother's bell will be resounding over the Stanford campus and other parts of Palo Alto, as a gift of eternity from my sister. Mother seems to like her bell, though she is disappointed that no one knows exactly when the Hoover Tower carillon will play.

"You didn't love me," I said to her, in a factual way on the phone.

"You just decided I didn't love you," she said, with a little laugh.

"Someone new likes me," I said. "He tells me I'm a perpetual teen-age prayer."

Mother was silent.

"I can say 'Puppy Sue, Puppy Sue,' midsentence, the way I always have, and he says 'Puppy Sue, Puppy Sue' back to me, and goes on with what he was saying."

Mother seemed to be listening.

"I found him a Dutch psychiatrist," I said.

"His psychiatrist will cure him of you," Mother cautioned, laughing merrily. "That's a terrible thing to say," she added. And then, "I wish you could tell Dr. Cederquist."

I had a bad moment. "I look good now," I said, after it had passed.

"You looked good the minute you were born," Mother said. She had never said such a thing to me before. Then she went on, "You cost twenty-five dollars, because your father was a doctor." This was an ancient family story that was always illustrated with a copy of the bill from Stanford Hospital. She told a story about her first dog, a wire-haired terrier. "My mother didn't believe in sleeping with dogs," she said, as a grave pronouncement. When Mother had been a little girl, in San Francisco, her father, in quiet slippers, had carried the dog into her bedroom late at night, so it could sleep on Mother's bed. In the mornings, before my grandmother was awake, my grandfather (he died when Mother was twelve) would sneak into her bedroom and carry the dog back to its basket, off the kitchen. Then she went on to talk about Snowball Brown, a rabbit she'd had as a child. She sounds a little sad, for her, whenever she talks about Snowball Brown (animals matter), so I didn't say anything.

"Do you want to know what I had for lunch?" she asked then. "Round whole-wheat crackers with peanut butter. It's only good with currant jelly. It's Mary Ellen or something. Remember Mary Ellen?"

I said I did: a California brand of jelly.

"I'm sure it comes in your grocery store," she assured me.

After a small lapse in the conversation, I asked her what she was thinking about.

"The flu epidemic of 1919 in San Francisco," she said. "We had to wear white cotton masks, pink silk on Saturday."

"Where did you get the silk? From lingerie?"

"No, no, my mother bought them"—a slight reprimand. "In a department store, I suppose. You bought them the way you would a petticoat. I was sent down to San Mateo to live with friends of my mother—you were safe there," she said.

"I don't know anyone nice except this new friend who likes me," I said. I don't know why I said that.

"You say you don't know any nice people. I'll tell you something nice: I just gave Follie"—her second gray poodle of that name—"a peanut ball. Goodbye, darling. Write that paper." Then she hung up.

After a minute I called her back.

"Why did you say that I 'ought to be put to sleep for a while,' after I told you I didn't feel real? When I was eight."

She didn't say anything, but not, I think, because anything I say could be a surprise to her. "It was in your dressing room in Palo Alto," I said.

"If I were you, I would shoot me," she said, in a tone of more irony than George Trow has ever mustered. And then, before she put the receiver down, "*À bientôt,* as we say in French."

. . .

Mary Ann sounded just like Mary Ann—most like I've remembered her—when she answered the telephone: calm. She talked slowly, as if she were completely there, not thinking of some other thing. Even the way she said hello was calm, and patient, and she seemed to like my calling her, which was a comfort. It was 1996—forty-one years since she'd left my father's office and our house—and she said, after I'd told her her voice sounded the same, "Well, yours doesn't."

She said she was living in the middle of six acres of oak trees in a glass house with real wild animals passing by, and with seven cats inside. She said she'd had the main door made "wide enough for a wheelchair, in case I ever need one." Mary Ann was always levelheaded, earnest, inventive. I could feel exactly what it had been like to *be* with Mary Ann.

I asked her if she remembered the day in the kitchen—I was nine—when I asked her if I would, all my life until I died, remember that exact moment: just me and her in the kitchen in Palo Alto leaning against the refrigerator, Mary Ann nearer the sink with sweater set, straight skirt, good posture. She had said to me that she didn't know for certain if I would remember it or not.

Now, on the telephone in the middle of her oak trees, she said, "I do remember"—and it seemed as if we remembered it in just the same way.

"What ever happened to Noel?" she asked. Noel was the medium-sized black poodle who really liked my sister and kind of hated me. Mary Ann remembered the names of all the animals that had been in our house. "Devoted," Mary Ann said of Noel. "I remember the day Belinda got her."

After a silence, Mary Ann said, as if she'd saved a special present for me, "Remember when we went to the drive-in movies? Your parents were in Europe, and I'd bring you home on Fridays—you were boarding—and we'd go to a drive-in movie. You used to take Bambi and get all wrapped up in a blanket and I don't remember what we'd see."

I do. We saw the musical *Seven Brides for Seven Brothers,* for one. Jane Powell was in it. And Howard Keel. In the end the seven boys and girls sang and danced and got married.

"Remember Amber?" I said. She'd been my little yellow cat, a blonde, my favorite.

"Ambi," Mary Ann sort of corrected me. "We called her Ambi."

"One night at the dinner table, my sister told me Amber had been 'mentally ill' before she died," I said. Mary Ann laughed. It was a real, amused laugh, though soft.

She said now, "I remember going over to your house to watch the coronation of the Queen on TV. It was the first TV I ever saw. Nineteen fifty-two. I can't remember where it was."

"In the garden room," I said.

While I was talking to Mary Ann on the telephone there were silences. But none of her silences made me feel they were the end of the conversation or that I had said the wrong thing.

"I remember the time the living-room carpet was taken up and dyed dog-spot brown," she said now. "Your mother couldn't stand the dog spots anymore." This was her only reference to Mother.

"I thought I would get an answering machine when I called you," I said, "and I'd say 'Alison Rose called' and you'd never call me back."

"I would have called you back instantly," she said.

We'd been talking for perhaps an hour when I said, in the context of I forget what and kind of racing through it, "My father said I was crazy."

Mary Ann said, "It wasn't because he thought you were crazy." She went on, "He had very little empathy. He didn't know how it must be for the other person. It was the fact he didn't feel what they were feeling." And, "He couldn't feel what it was like to be that person."

There was a pause. "I didn't exactly feel sorry for you . . . but I could see you were not going to take life easily. In a way, you were sort of like him. He tended to fight things he couldn't handle. I remember you two going at it."

"Did *you* think I was crazy?" I asked.

"Good heavens, no," she said.

"I never got married or anything," I said. "I guess I never did find anyone." Then I asked her, "Did you ever find anyone?"

"I did find him once," she said, "but he died and that was a long time ago." I didn't think she meant my father, and I didn't ask.

I asked her instead, "Do you like the humans?"

And Mary Ann said, "They have their place."

. . .

Last October, after more than a year of telephone calls, I boarded the animals and got on an airplane and flew to see Gardner McKay. I just wanted to see him before he died, and he'd said I could come. It was odd to hear the ukulele music piped in at the Honolulu airport, where Madeleine, Gardner's Irish wife, met me in her car, curbside. When I got in the car, Madeleine put a lei around my neck, pink flowers with white, as if it had been made just for me. The lei had a strong scent of jasmine. We drove to the house, about eleven miles on a highway.

"I knew you would come," Madeleine said.

More than a year before, Gardner had sent me a letter; in the mailbox, the brown envelope with his wildcat rubber-stamped on it: a little shock. Four years before that, we'd had a fight about something he'd thought I'd meant to do; four years of silence. Now I read his letter right by the mailbox. He was writing to say he had cancer: "If I don't hear from you I'll think something is terribly wrong." He signed it, "Love as before." I went upstairs and dialed his number on Oahu. I still knew it by heart. He answered. In that conversation, he asked me if I would like him to send me the old rag doll he had that had belonged to Francine. He'd called her Tristine, for *tristesse* and Francine. The moment when hanging up was about to happen, I said, in a nervous hurry, *"Je t'aime."*

"Je t'aime aussi," he said, in no rush, just slowly and plain.

Other telephone conversations were largely about his child-hood. He had made friends with a fat boy when he was growing up in the South of France. When his mother found out, she refused to let Gardner play with him. "I went from the people who think they're worthless to the animals," he said. We talked about the animals. The lions and the cheetahs of Lizard Court were a thing of the past. For years now, Gardner had had only an orange cat named Jimmy G. He'd taken a photograph of Jimmy G. and sent it to me.

Gardner was dying in a small room downstairs in his and Madeleine's house, with Jimmy G. beside him on the bed. Jimmy G. had only one eye, because of a tumor; the bad eye had been sewn shut. Madeleine would do anything so that Jimmy G. would stay with Gardner until he died. Jimmy G. wasn't allowed to die first.

Gardner was certainly close to dying, but he was alive enough to say, when I stood at the foot of his bed and he saw that I was actually there, "You're beautiful. I love you." I wasn't completely late.

"Come near, be close," he said. I had already sat down on one edge of the white sheets of his rented hospital bed, halfway between his face and the foot of the bed, and I was holding his hand. I could feel the force of his hand not letting go of mine. I turned to look at Madeleine, who was sitting nearby in a chair against the wall. It was a small room. Her face seemed to say everything was O.K., so I moved up closer to Gardner, took his right hand in both of mine, and leaned over to kiss him on his lips—just the way I kissed Toast before she died, was how the kiss turned out.

"Now we're never going to have the conversation we'll never have," Gardner said. He didn't lift his head off the pillow. He spoke slowly, the way he had on the telephone. No agitation. Over the years, a sense of agitation or impatience had been in his voice more often than not, but now I didn't hear it.

I would be sleeping on a large daybed in the living room, since Madeleine's brother, Brian, had the spare bedroom. Brian and Madeleine were Gardner's caretakers. And his protectors—his angels, I thought. Definitely. The daybed overlooked three strong palm trees that were far taller than the rest of the trees in the landscape, their branches swaying the way branches do under black clouds with some blue sky over them; a partial tropical sunset at 6:20 p.m. The Pacific Ocean was out there, visible past the palm trees. I spent time sitting on the daybed counting the branches on these three tallest palm trees, about thirteen branches on each, and listening to the ocean. The next morning, Madeleine told me that from there you can't hear the ocean, so it wasn't the ocean that I had heard after all—it was the wind. During the days I was there, when Madeleine wasn't watching over Gardner, Brian was. Madeleine cooked the rest of the time, so I stayed with her in the kitchen, or we sat together at the kitchen table, in front of a window jammed with palm trees, like a jungle out there.

Down below, not many feet from a swimming pool, was Gardner's work house, for his writing. He had just had it built. In the dark, it looked turquoise, but was actually dark green, with a copper roof that could look pale blue, depending on the light.

In the whole big house, in the nicest way, in my head I was still in my room at home. I didn't spend so very much time in Gardner's room downstairs, for reasons of tacit modesty, but, knowing that Gardner was in his room downstairs, I felt as safe in that house as I had felt in my room in Palo Alto, with the television on, with him inside it; as safe as I had felt later up on Coldwater Canyon in Lizard Court. Not a trespasser, or even in on a pass.

And yet: there are thirty different kinds of palm trees in Hawaii. Over the three and a half days I spent there, I took rolls of photographs of palm trees, the three tallest in the yard, and some shorter ones with yellow leaves. I lay down on the ground on my back to do this.

"It's tremendously sunny outside," I said to Brian when he came into the kitchen. "I don't remember ever seeing so much light."

"We hate the darkness," Brian said. By "we" he meant the Irish. Brian seemed never to stop moving up and down the stairs, with something to drink for Gardner. He was in near-constant motion doing this and anything else for Gardner.

"I come from a fairly sunny place, more or less, California," I said, "so I don't hate darkness the same way you do. But I do hate it."

Brian and Madeleine looked alike. Tall, lanky, thin. Brian was six feet two, more lithe than lanky sometimes. His legs were long and narrow, like a boy's, though he was forty-five. His nose was long and straight, his wavy hair a strawberry blond. There was lots of it. He had a narrow face and blue eyes, that Irish skin. He was one of the prettiest sad men I had ever met. He was like a present from Gardner. He made me an orange juice now, squeezing the oranges himself. I asked him if there was any chance we could go to the beach the next day, so I could see the turquoise water up close, just for a little while.

Brian and I went downstairs, where Madeleine was in the room with Gardner. I held one of Gardner's hands with both of mine. Madeleine was sitting on the hospital bed, too. "You two look beautiful," Gardner said to Madeleine and me, as if he firmly believed it.

"It's the light," Madeleine said.

"You stay," Gardner said to the three of us.

No matter how thin he was from being sick, Gardner's frame was large. His head was gorgeous and large, and so was the rest of him. Maybe his nose is thinner, I thought, a bit narrower; but the beauty can't be wrecked.

Brian said, in his low-key, factual tone, that we could take the trip to the ocean the next day, that Madeleine would stay with Gardner for a few hours. When Brian and I left Gardner's room, I went back upstairs and sat on the daybed. Madeleine's paintings of Gardner were in this room: one was of Gardner sitting in a chair, slumped over to one side. In all of them Gardner was big and sad, the colors browns and grays, dark.

"There's the beach where they filmed *From Here to Eternity*," Brian said. It was a small, small beach. No one was there. George had once declared that I had needed "Jesus, Harold Brodkey, Gardner McKay, and Burt Lancaster to make it through," and I remembered that now. Brian kept on driving.

We walked over sandbags to get to the sand on another beach, where we could sit down. Brian said I should have a photograph of myself walking along the sandbags, in my pink-and-white striped skirt and black T-shirt, carrying my notebook (I'm never without my notebook), with my red bag over my shoulder.

"*Adventures in Paradise,*" I said to myself, I couldn't help it. I laughed. I had to laugh once. Brian took my photograph on the beach itself. I was holding on to my notebook. He held my red bag.

"Gardner loves you," Brian said. We were looking straight ahead at the water, which was indeed turquoise, and also aquamarine and marine blue, with some white waves. I didn't say anything.

"I wanted to see you as Gardner saw you," he said. "That's what I looked for in you when I met you," and he said it as if he'd seen whatever that was immediately. I lived for what he was saying, literally. It was everything I wanted to hear. As soon as I heard it, it became the only thing I was thinking about.

"There's a rainbow, but it's hard to see," Brian said. I looked hard. Now there were two rainbows. "A rainbow and its half sister," Brian said. The half sister was a taller, somewhat brighter rainbow in the fog. That's what he meant.

A frigate bird was gliding along when the sky turned all gray.

Brian had been making calls to Madeleine from his cell phone, in case she needed him. Now he told her we were on our way home.

"I could take advantage of you," I said to him right then.

"I wish you would," he said.

. . .

Back at the house, Madeleine sat with Gardner while Brian xeroxed stories of mine that Gardner had asked me to bring for him to read. That night, Madeleine and I sat on the upstairs terrace, where she told me tale after tale about growing up in Ireland. She also said, "I knew you just wanted to see him." Gardner was dying downstairs below us. Not dying at that precise moment, but dying.

The morning of the day I was leaving, Gardner was asleep. Madeleine and Brian and I were gathered around a green table by the pool outside his room. The glass door was open. We could all see in.

Madeleine was beginning to cut her brother's hair with a scissors, lifting wet pieces of it with a comb, then cutting at an angle. Jimmy G. was sitting in a chair at the table, watching with his one good eye.

"He has a glass in his hand," Brian said. He was mindful of Gardner all the time. The glass looked as if it might slip out of Gardner's hand, fall on the floor. Brian said, gently, "Why don't you go in his room and take the glass out of his hand, Alison." His Irish accent was strong. He knew I'd been afraid to say goodbye. Madeleine was concentrating on the haircut.

I went into Gardner's room. I wanted to and I didn't. I was afraid I would startle him, that he might wake up. What would I say? Would he die? I didn't want him to die while I was watching him. I didn't want to embarrass him. I took the glass out of Gardner's big hand and put it on a table. He didn't wake up. He was still my old friend Antelope.

Outside, Madeleine was hovering over her brother, devotedly cutting his hair—carefully. Just for a minute, it was as if the three of us had grown up together in the same house, Madeleine and I fussing about Brian's hair: "What about here?" "A little shorter here?" "Oh, it looks good."

We were all keeping an eye on Gardner.

"What movie star does Brian look like?" I said to Madeleine. "Lawrence of Arabia?"

"You mean Peter O'Toole," Madeleine said.

"What about the one in that movie with all the boys running in Europe?"

"Scottish," Brian said.

"Yes, the blond. You look like him," I said.

Brian's hair was getting shorter and shorter. "Go in and tell him you're leaving in fifteen minutes," Madeleine said to me.

I went in. He woke up. His face looked alert, and happy when I said I'd left him the stories he'd asked for. But seconds later his head fell back and he looked like a dying man again. I sat on the bed and held his hand, which that morning had wires, tubes, and needles in it. I hesitated before doing this—to see if it was O.K. with him. I couldn't altogether tell, but I kissed him anyway. "I love you," I said. His eyes were closed. Then I said, "I'll talk to you," which sounded awkward to me because I wouldn't be talking to him. We would never say what we were never going to say, whatever it was, you could tell. "I'll talk to you," I heard myself say again. "It's not all that stupid, what you said," I told myself. I wished that I would be talking to him, though. Jimmy G. was stretched out next to Gardner. Faithful.

Madeleine and I said goodbye with our arms around each other by the front door. She felt tall and angular and thin and muscular; like Gardner's wife. The pink-and-white lei had dried out on the lamp where I had hung it, next to the daybed. I was going to take it with me, but Madeleine said she couldn't bear it if I did—"like Miss Havisham," she said. She wouldn't let me take it.

"The birds are loud," Brian said on the way to the airport. It was 5:45 p.m. "They're loud every night," he said, "fighting for their places in the trees—to spend the night."

He was making a detour, though I didn't know it was a detour, to a stall selling leis, called Harriet's. He got out of the car and before long came back with a huge, a masculine lei, with darker colors: crimson, not pink. He put it around my neck and I didn't take it off until I was in my room in New York.

.   .   .

A man I know—not a brisk, blond person but one who, though he functions more than well enough, regularly suffers from dullness and darkness and bad-thinking spirits from Hell— this man said the other day over the telephone from Chicago, "I want to put a bullet through my head to let a breeze in." I know what he means, but what I like better is the last drawing Harold made for me in my Trow-Rose office at School. He picked up my black Pentel and, leaning over my shoulder, drew a bird flying faster than normal bird-flight, with downward-slanting lines for fierce eyes and a beak. Under the bird, with thick wavy lines, he made an ocean. Right now I forget how he drew the sky, but there is one: placid. He handed the black Pentel back to me and said with nearly stoic affection, "Bird Complaining Over the North Atlantic."

He waited while I wrote down what he'd said at the top of the white piece of typing paper. George had said that I was "rescued by my own actions and didn't get killed"—which is true, absolutely. Harold took a slightly different slant on the subject with his declaration that goes, "People don't like to be outshone. They'll kill you if it bothers them enough."

Two weeks later, Brian called me here to say that Gardner had died. He left two messages. Gardner had died only minutes before he called the first time, and when I reached him he told me both he and Madeleine had been right by Gardner's side. Just before he died, Brian told me, Gardner said to the two of them, "Yell like Indians."